It's Our School, It's Our T

To dear Julia
with love,
Geraldine
_x x_

It's Our School, It's Our Time outlines a whole-school approach to teacher–pupil collaboration, illustrating how aspects of social inequality can be addressed by involvement in the school community and active participation in decision-making from an early age. The book presents insights into the psychological processes that are at work when pupils and teachers share decision-making, and how this can harness and increase motivation for teachers and their pupils.

Combining both theory and examples of practice, this book provides clarity about the impact of collaborative decision-making and how it can help pupils to take ownership of their classrooms and promote greater co-operation and productivity. This book:

- draws on 25 stories from Dr Rowe's own study and experiences as an educational psychologist, and the accounts of other educators and researchers.
- shows how teachers and school leaders have overcome some common hurdles that those in conventional schools might encounter.
- provides research-evidence and practical examples from real-life classrooms that will inspire teachers, teaching assistants and school leaders.

Written by a highly experienced educational psychologist, this companion guide will help teachers, head teachers, teacher educators and student teachers to transform achievement, behaviour and motivation through greater collaboration with their pupils.

Dr Geraldine Rowe has worked as an Educational Psychologist for over 30 years in several UK Local Authorities, in over 100 schools, nurseries and colleges. Her website is www.pupilparticipation.co.uk.

It's Our School, It's Our Time

A Companion Guide to Whole-School Collaborative Decision-Making

Geraldine Rowe

Routledge
Taylor & Francis Group

LONDON AND NEW YORK

First published 2021
by Routledge
2 Park Square, Milton Park, Abingdon, Oxon OX14 4RN

and by Routledge
52 Vanderbilt Avenue, New York, NY 10017

Routledge is an imprint of the Taylor & Francis Group, an informa business

British Library Cataloguing-in-Publication Data
A catalogue record for this book is available from the British Library

Library of Congress Cataloging-in-Publication Data
Names: Rowe, Geraldine, author.
Title: It's our school, it's our time : a companion guide to whole-school
collaborative decision-making/Geraldine Rowe.
Identifiers: LCCN 2020024456 | ISBN 9780367859343 (hardback) | ISBN
9780367859381 (paperback) | ISBN 9781003015864 (ebook)
Subjects: LCSH: Student participation in curriculum planning. | Curriculum
planning–Decision making. | Educational equalization. | School
management and organization–Decision making. | Teacher-student relationships.
Classification: LCC LB2806.15 .R68 2021 | DDC 375/.001–dc23
LC record available at https://lccn.loc.gov/2020024456

ISBN: 978-0-367-85934-3 (hbk)
ISBN: 978-0-367-85938-1 (pbk)
ISBN: 978-1-003-01586-4 (ebk)

Typeset in Bembo and Helvetica Neue LT Pro
by KnowledgeWorks Global Ltd.

To Jeremy

Contents

Preface

This book is about how teachers and pupils of all ages and backgrounds can collaborate to make important decisions about what goes on in their schools and classrooms. It is a book for head teachers, teachers, teaching assistants, pupil teachers and professionals involved in schools and educational policy at local, national and international levels.

This book is not about school councils or one-off consultations with pupils; it is about how teachers and pupils collaborate in decisions that affect the whole class and the whole school. These decisions may be about curriculum, discipline, the environment or resource and time management. I believe that of all aspects of pupil voice, collaborative decision-making (CDM) has the potential to make the greatest impact on well-being and educational outcomes. It is also an area where substantial change has yet to take place in schools.

As you read this book, I invite you to reflect on the following questions: Why do you want to collaborate with your pupils? How can you bridge the gap with colleagues who are yet to be convinced? And, finally, what are you prepared to change, sacrifice, invest, add, stop or learn in order to make your teaching, leading and policy-making truly collaborative?

Very little has been written on the teacher experience of decision-making, and even fewer books offer guidance to teachers who want to share decision-making with their pupils. In my doctoral research into teacher–pupil collaboration in the primary classroom, I studied three teachers to find out what it is like for them to pursue approaches that bring pupils into the decision-making process in their classrooms. My own research was an attempt to find out first-hand from teachers why they value CDM, their perceptions of what makes it possible to teach in a more collaborative way and what obstacles they have encountered. By spending time with these teachers and listening to them talk about their experiences of collaboration, I was able to gain insight into their professional lives, the complexity of relationships with the class and the influences exerted by the opinions and decisions of school leaders and policy-makers.

I learned many things about collaboration in the classroom from the teacher's perspective. Even for those teachers who have a strong faith in children's ability to take responsibility for their own decisions, it requires patience and persistence to teach in this way. The more I learnt about the experiences of these teachers, the more my admiration grew for all teachers who manage even small breakthrough explorations into this form of shared decision-making in schools with non-collaborative cultures. I came to realise that CDM in the classroom is a much more subtle art than I had previously imagined. I also learned that many of the problems faced by the teachers in my study came about because they were trying to teach in a collaborative way, in schools where the culture was essentially non-collaborative.

I concluded that more examples of collaborative practice and guidance were needed to help practitioners to work in this way. Throughout this book you will find stories and examples of CDM from my doctoral study, my observations in schools I have visited and worked in and written reports about practice in other schools. My research also convinced me that CDM has a much greater chance of thriving if it is introduced as a whole-school approach and becomes part of the school culture, which is why I have dedicated a whole chapter to Leadership and Culture. Even if you thoroughly approve of involving children in decision-making, you may feel that this is only possible in small classes with high-achieving and well-behaved children with highly supportive parents. Fortunately, for those teachers wanting to try CDM, there is a rich, international, tradition of progressive, collaborative and democratic education to show that collaborative approaches work for children from the most disadvantaged sectors of society to the most privileged. Research into more participative approaches to teaching suggests that all children benefit from CDM, but those who benefit the most are those from disadvantaged homes.

Throughout this book you will find real-life stories about teachers who have used CDM with their pupils; lessons are drawn from each example, and suggestions are given for things to try out. Some of these stories are drawn from my own research and extensive experience in UK schools. Further examples have been selected from the accounts of other educators and researchers in the UK and other countries.

A word about the title of this book: the title of my thesis, *It's their school; it's their time*, combines quotes from two of the teachers participating in my study, explaining why they involved their pupils in CDM. The reason I adapted the title for this book is that one of the important messages in my thesis is that for CDM to flourish, *teachers* also need a voice. Teachers who have never tried sharing decision-making with their pupils may be fearful of losing control and of handing over all of their power to the class. I wanted a title that reassured them that this book describes a *joint venture* between teachers and pupils, not the complete transfer of power from teachers to children.

When I was thinking about the audience for this book, I thought not only of those professionals listed above, but also of teenage (or younger) readers who may be interested in exploring educational possibilities for themselves – I would love it if pupils and teachers were to read this book together and transform their classroom experience into one characterised by ownership, community and high motivation. With this readership in mind, I have attempted to avoid jargon and adopt a conversational tone. I hope that, even though my writing may sometimes come across as casual, readers won't interpret my writing as in any way condescending or unprofessional; it is certainly not meant to be either.

My ideas have been informed and influenced by what I have read as well as what I've learned through observation, discussions and reflection. There are some ideas which I have now made so much my own that I have forgotten where I first came across them, and I hope that those writers and researchers who inspired me will forgive me for this, or contact me to put me right. However, where I can, I will tell you where I got my ideas or stories from, unless of course they are drawn from my own experience, which I make clear at the time.

At the start of this Preface, I invited you to consider some questions. Actually, it would be even better if, as you read, you talk to your colleagues, pupils and friends and make a note of questions you all really want to find the answers to. As one of the key messages of collaboration is that 'those who own the questions will be most excited by the answers', we might as well start as we mean to go on.

Acknowledgements

Thanks go to you, my family: Jeremy, for your love, for your belief in me, for giving me the time and space to write, for never asking me to do jobs when I am at home writing and for cooking at weekends; Francesca, for your art, and for reminding me to think of my readers; Naomi, for many collaborative conversations and for keeping my feet firmly on the ground with your teacher's creativity; Martin, who just 'gets it' and encourages me to be bold; and young Zachary for bringing us all such joy.

It's been wonderful to have you, my neighbours and friends from the choir and the rowing club, showing such sincere interest in my writing over all these months – we'll have to find something else to talk about over coffee now. Those friends who came over to the house to workshop book excerpts probably don't appreciate just how helpful you were, so thank you, Catherine, Elaine, Suzie, Angela, Rosie, Alexa, Helen C.and Maggie.

For my interest in pupil voice and participation, I have to thank my late parents, Margaret, who was the kind of teacher who could always see the good in her pupils, and Gerard, for bringing out the 'square peg' in me.

In my first year as a Psychology student at UWIST, Cardiff, I met and volunteered alongside Jo Ford, a retired social worker and founding member of the charity then known as 'Voice of the Child in Care' (now 'Coram Voice'). Jo worked to ensure that all children, especially those 'in care', had a voice. Later, during my professional EP training, I was introduced to Albert Kushlik, a retired physician who campaigned for the participation and inclusion rights of disabled children and young people, and who put his beliefs into practice, making it possible for children with severe disabilities to be educated near their families and sharing his own home with a disabled student. These two individuals showed me the importance of children's and young people's participation in decision-making. They also taught me that anyone who supports children and young people in this way needs to be prepared to challenge accepted 'institutional' traditions, and to expect opposition to their ideas. Thank you, Jo and Albert, wherever you are.

One of the reasons why I chose to do my doctorate at the Institute of Education was that Professor Michael Fielding was there. Although he had retired just before I got there, we met a few times and he introduced me to this country's rich tradition of progressive and democratic education. Through Michael, I met the inspirational Derry Hannam, who has given me great encouragement for my writing. Thank you, Michael and Derry. Also, I want to thank Nazlin Bhimani, brilliant Librarian at the Newsam Library at the Institute of Education for introducing me to new literatures around collaborative and progressive education, and for showing great interest in my research.

Thank you, Dr Ivan Honey, Professor Liz Todd and Dame Alison Peacock for your generous feedback on my book proposal. Your belief in this book gave me the courage to keep going.

And finally, thank you to the teachers and pupils who participated in my study and to those teachers, head teachers and pupils who have taught me, through example and conversations, that CDM is not only possible in regular state schools, but that it is essential.

AMDG

Introduction

Decision-making is something teachers know a lot about. I mean a *lot*. Before lessons even begin, teachers are making decisions about curriculum, materials, teaching and learning activities, seating, timetabling, differentiation, motivation and so on. Then once lessons are underway there are thousands of minute-by-minute decisions about pace, revision of concepts, responses to individual pupils, how and how much to assist, as well as decisions about classroom discipline. All these decisions, whilst also trying to give pupils a love of learning, excellent academic attainments and promoting good mental health. Phew!

At the same time, pupils are making *their own* decisions. They are deciding whether to listen to the teacher or investigate the woodlouse they have just found; whether to struggle on or ask for help; how to start their writing; whether to aim to complete five questions or be content with three. These decisions are usually about their own behaviour and learning, and they may be unaware that they are even making these decisions. Because decision-making tends to be an invisible process, learning how to make *better* decisions can be a haphazard process. You will not be surprised to know that children from poor homes, where planning for short-term survival is the priority, may be used to a very different kind of decision-making than those from better off families. If they don't expand their decision-making skills, they may end up making decisions for themselves that keep them poor. Wouldn't it be great if it was possible to help all pupils to become skilled decision-makers and improve their resilience and well-being at the same time? Maybe there is a way.

What is collaborative decision-making (CDM)?

Collaborative Decision-Making (CDM) is what happens when teachers and pupils make decisions together that affect the whole class or school. These decisions may be about community, curriculum, learning, recreation, discipline, the environment or resource and time management. CDM elevates decision-making to a curriculum outcome in its own right and one that involves the whole class and the teacher. It is explicit, public and social. Decisions become things to discuss and debate, and decision-making is no longer something done in other people's heads but something to discuss, to study; a skill to practice.

Maybe you've never called it CDM, but hopefully by the end of this book you will recognise it when you see it. You were using CDM when you invited your class to decide with you the topic of their forthcoming assembly; when you involved them in deciding which author to invite to talk to the class; when you planned the end-of-unit assessments together; when you debated and came up with solutions to the dirty floor in the changing room, or an alternative to queuing up in the rain. Perhaps you think it is enough just to do this once in a while, but can't really see how it would work as a complete philosophy for the many decisions that have to be made in the classroom. Or you may believe that, along with other pupil voice initiatives, there is a time and place for such things, but you would need some persuading to involve pupils in classroom decision-making on a regular basis.

Why classroom decision-making?

These days, most schools have some type of school council, consisting of a small number of pupil representatives who are selected through a mixture of teacher judgement and votes from fellow pupils. The involvement of school council members in school decision-making varies massively from school to school, but it is generally recognised that there are some great benefits for those pupils involved: improved confidence and skills in communication and leadership, and in decision-making processes; and opportunities to relate to members of staff on a more equal footing.

If learning how to make decisions in a community, and having the opportunity to contribute to that decision-making on a regular basis is valuable, then it needs to be available to all pupils, not just the few selected for these councils and schemes. Those children who never get chosen to represent the class may be the very pupils who most need these experiences and need to be helped to learn the skills of civic decision-making.

It has been proposed that representatives for student councils and similar student bodies are selected by lottery, so that everyone has an equal chance of being involved in school decision-making (Pek, Kennedy, & Cronkright, 2018). I go a step further and say that the way for all pupils to get these experiences on a daily basis is by *every* pupil taking part in collective decision-making about what goes on in their own classrooms.

Teachers I work with, in my role as Educational Psychologist (EP), often invite me into their lessons. When I visit classrooms, I am interested in what I can see going on, but I am even more interested in what pupils have to say about their motivation and expectations; the way in which they help and seek help from adults and fellow pupils; and how they use their classroom resources. I am especially interested in the social psychology of the class,– how people interact with each other and the ways in which people support each other. I have been in classrooms where you can clearly see pupils helping each other, and places where pupils are encouraged to focus solely on how well they are doing personally, irrespective of the needs of those around them.

As a newly qualified EP, my attention was captured by those practitioners and head teachers who talked with great respect about their pupils, and treated them as if their views really mattered. One such teacher, Deirdre, involved the four- and five-year-olds in her class to design a welcoming and inclusive environment for a new pupil with Down's syndrome. In another school, some Early Years practitioners were reviewing some long-established practices to see if they reflected an underestimation of children's skills. They held class discussions with the three- and four-year-olds about how they might do things for themselves that the grown-ups did for them at present. The children asked if they could pour drinks for each other instead of the grown-ups doing it. They said that they enjoyed using teapots in water play and felt confident that if a container had a spout, and wasn't too heavy, they could do the job themselves. It was a delight to watch these tiny children getting their teapots and toy watering cans filled and going round to serve their friends. It was messy to begin with, but the children helped to clean up spills.

Examples like these helped me to see that even very young children have the capacity and motivation to contribute to decisions about what goes on in their own classroom, and of the many potential opportunities to include children in decision-making. I started to wonder what classrooms might look like if we really were making the most of the skills and interests of pupils. I concluded that we weren't even scratching the surface. The more teachers I met who collaborated with their pupils, the more critical and less satisfied I became with classrooms where children's own skills, motivation and knowledge were ignored or undervalued in classroom planning and decision-making.

A few years ago, I led a Students-as-Researchers project in a London secondary school. Although the school had both male and female pupils, the student-researchers in this study were drawn from a group of boys identified as at risk of exclusion. As part of their research, the pupils interviewed teachers to find out about their most enjoyable teaching experiences. The research involved the student-researchers observing lessons and interviewing teachers and fellow pupils in their secondary school. Both the teachers and pupils enjoyed the interview experience, and reported that some of their most memorable and enjoyable times in the classroom were those involving humour and unexpected events, usually initiated by pupils.

These results suggested that a level of fun, variety and unpredictability is an important way to maintain classroom motivation and engagement, and that 30 pupils are more likely to provide that element than a single teacher. Through the interviews, teachers shared their personal stories of classroom experiences and perceptions with the student-researchers. This gave the boys an appreciation of what lessons can be like for teachers. When this was combined with classroom observations to identify what pupils did that helped others to enjoy and learn, they started to analyse what was going on. In a final focus group, it was clear that the student-researchers had been affected by the experience. One the student-researchers, reflecting on the behaviour of fellow pupils, commented, 'It's the students that need to change, not the teachers' (Rowe, 2015). This occasion also gave them space to reflect on their own perceptions of school. Our discussion wandered into the realms of how the experience of being researchers had altered their perception of school. One of the chattier student-researcher had gone quiet for a bit, so I asked him if he was okay. He had obviously been thinking about our whole discussion and said, after a pause, 'Do you know, we've been here for so long, we've forgotten *why* we're here.' I wish that his teachers had been present to hear this. I don't think he is the only 14-year-old who feels this way.

The teachers and boys who were involved obviously enjoyed talking to each other and gained increased respect in the process. The boys saw their own behaviour from a new angle and the teachers were pleasantly surprised at how enjoyable they found conversing about their work with the student-researchers. The perceptiveness of these student-researchers, all of whom had issues of behaviour and disaffection, and their suggestions regarding ways to improve classroom life motivated me to continue to keep pupil participation as the main focus for my doctoral thesis, a couple of years later (Rowe, 2018).

It will come as no surprise to learn that pupils are seasoned observers of teacher behaviour. What may be surprising to some is the empathy that some seemingly difficult pupils have for their teachers. This Students-as-Researchers project unearthed the empathy that seemingly disruptive boys had for their long-suffering teachers; the moving way in which pupils described their experiences; the dreadful lack of opportunity for them to do so; the needless fear some teachers had of these boys; and the waste of the ability that these boys showed that they possess. These boys were highly marginalised in that they were rarely taught alongside their peers in the classroom. Their eagerness to take part in lessons where they were acting as observers – and as such were asked to refrain from engaging in the lesson – was unexpected, as was their eloquence and understanding of their own and other pupils' daily experiences. It really reminded me that it is only by involving the least desirable pupils in discussions and decision-making that our schools can become socially inclusive (Rowe, 2015).

> It is often considered a crime for one child to help another in his schoolwork.
> John Dewey, the 'father' of democratic education, on the lack of community spirit in classrooms (Dewey, 1915).

It doesn't make sense that teachers are working overtime and taking on all of the responsibility for planning and preparation themselves rather than involving pupils in these valuable educational tasks. Your pupils have free time, they have ideas, they have seven- and eight-year-old (or 17–18-year-old) brains and can tell you what would interest them and their friends. Why do it all yourself?

Collaboration as a valuable commodity

In industry and health, it has been recognised that the involvement of consumers is central to design, not only because this partnership improves the quality of the products and services, but that when consumers invest time and thought into design, it gives them a psychological sense of ownership and loyalty. Medical practitioners are starting to acknowledge the important role that CDM can play in the treatment of children with chronic health conditions. They have noticed that those children whose parents collaborate with them to make medical decisions about treatment not only go on to develop decision-making skills as a result, but that treatments planned in collaboration with child patients are more likely to be adhered to (Miller, 2009).

When Great Ormond Street Hospital gave children as young as four years of age the opportunity to decide how much pain relief they needed, doctors were surprised to discover that the doses the children selected were either the same, or lower than those they would have prescribed. If children this young can make judgements on their own medication, what other decisions could they make, which adults are currently making for them (Llewellyn, 1993, in Miller, 1997)?

The involvement of pupils in the design of what goes on in their schools and classrooms can no longer be ignored. Attention has been drawn in recent years to the major inequalities in educational, health and economic outcomes for children from low income families, and the current focus on children's mental health and well-being further emphasises these inequalities. More than ever, teachers are looking for approaches that put learners' interests and motivation at the centre and offer a curriculum that is relevant to their pupils' lives whilst maintaining an ordered sense of community in the school.

CDM not only impacts on learning, behaviour, well-being and relationships between and amongst pupils and teachers, but also teaches pupils about collaboration, with the potential to impact the way they engage in decision-making in their future lives. Jacqueline Thousand, Professor of Education, argued that making collaborative decision-making in schools a voluntary option – something educational professionals can choose to do if they feel like it – is as crazy as suggesting that it is up to individual health-care professionals whether or not to collaborate in performing an operation, or providing post-operative care (Thousand, Villa, Paolucci-Whitcomb, & Nevin, 1992). She makes it clear that if collaboration is to be truly *respected* in schools, then it should be *expected* and *inspected*! I would add, that it needs to be *invested* in – preparation and training in particular. Practitioners will need a lot of support, but many will welcome the chance to become the kind of teachers they set out to be.

The continuing drive to reduce inequalities in educational and mental health outcomes for children from disadvantaged backgrounds calls for a new look at what is going on in our classrooms; children need the chance to become critical thinkers with a sense of power, entitlement and strong school-belonging. CDM will not solve all these problems, but without it, the outcomes will be sorely limited.

References

Dewey, J. (1915). *The school and society* (2nd ed.). Chicago & London: University of Chicago Press.

Llewellyn, N. (1993). The use of PCA for paediatric post-operative pain management. *Paediatric Nursing, 5*(5), 12–15.

Miller, J. (1997). *Never too young: How young children can take responsibility and make decisions.* London: National Early Years Network & Save the Children.

Miller, V. A. (2009). Parent–child collaborative decision making for the management of chronic illness: A qualitative analysis. *Fam Syst Health, 27*(3), 249–266.

Pek, S., Kennedy, J., & Cronkright, A. (2018). Democracy transformed: Perceived legitimacy of the institutional shift from election to random selection of representatives. *Journal of Public Deliberation, 14*(1). Article 3. Retrieved from https://www.researchgate.net/publication/326237185_Democracy_Transformed_Perceived_Legitimacy_of_the_Institutional_Shift_from_Election_to_Random_Selection_of_Representatives

Rowe, G. (2015). Students as Researchers into their own Classroom Climate: How appreciative inquiry changes perceptions. Unpublished report. UCL Institute of Education. Retrieved from: www.pupilparticipation.co.uk/resources

Rowe, G. (2018) Democracy in the primary classroom. Unpublished thesis. UCL Institute of Education. Retrieved from: www.pupilparticipation.co.uk/resources

Thousand, J., Villa, R., Paolucci-Whitcomb, P., & Nevin, A. (1992). A rationale and vision for collaborative consultation. In *Controversial issues confronting special education: Divergent perspectives.* (2nd ed.). Boston: Allyn & Bacon.

It is possible!
A study of three teachers

For all my working life, as a teacher and Educational Psychologist (EP), I have been aware of the importance of involving children and adolescents in decisions and have seen for myself the damaging effects that powerlessness and disaffection can have on children and adolescents. I've also witnessed the positive impact on achievement, fellowship and morale that comes from involving pupils in their own educational, social and behavioural plans. I've noticed that teachers who listen to and involve pupils in this way are also the teachers who get the most productivity and co-operation from pupils, particularly those with a history of deprivation and educational failure.

Why no collaborative decision-making (CDM) in classrooms?

Despite decades of research showing the benefits of pupil participation in decision-making, it is still rare to come across classrooms where this is happening. Rather than finding out more about why CDM is *not* happening, I used my doctoral research to search for teachers who were working in this way and study them (Rowe, 2018). I eventually found three teachers who were using some CDM in their classrooms some of the time, and who were willing to help me in my research. They were all working in conventional schools where this way of teaching was not the norm, and had developed this approach independently with their pupils. Over 15 months I explored the experiences of these three teachers who were involving their pupils in some collaborative decision-making.

I carried out multiple, in-depth interviews interspersed with classroom visits. Through this approach I hoped to gain a better understanding of what it is like to be a teacher using CDM in a regular state school. The three participants were interviewed over a period of 13, 8 and 5 months respectively, and data was analysed using Interpretative Phenomenological Analysis (IPA). IPA is a relatively new research methodology, involving an in-depth analysis of data from a small number of individuals who are all experiencing a similar phenomenon. The idea is that by researching in depth the experiences of a small number of individuals, a deeper insight is gained into the phenomenon participants are all experiencing – in this case, CDM.

The research aims were:

- To develop an understanding of what CDM looks like in the teaching environments of the participants;
- To understand how this practice develops;
- To understand the meaning that CDM holds for teachers;
- To understand the uniqueness, commonalities and divergences of teachers' experience of CDM; and
- To identify possible implications for education, policy and future research, based on these findings.

My participants

My particular research design meant that I needed to find three participants to study in depth over several months. My concerted efforts to find suitable participants through letters to schools, recommendations from friends and colleagues who work in schools and even setting up my own Pupil Participation Interest group, put me in touch with a dozen or so wonderful teachers, none of whom was actually using CDM with their pupils, although many expressed an interest in CDM. Most of these teachers involved their classes in regular discussions on slavery, values, human rights and the like, but rarely were discussions about pupils' own experiences of their classroom and school; about the way assemblies were organised; the benefits or otherwise of spelling tests; or their suggestions for next term's science curriculum. I knew that teachers using CDM were rare, but that they did exist, because I had occasionally come across them in my EP work in schools over the years and had also read about them and met them at meetings and conferences. Fortunately, as I was still going into schools I had daily contact with teachers, and in this way I was able to find my participants.

Once my research was underway I discovered why it had been so difficult to find participants through the normal recruitment channels: not only are teachers using CDM rare, but they would not necessarily have recognised that what they were doing had a name or was worthy of study. Indeed, all three teachers would occasionally give me a puzzled look and ask, 'Why are you so interested in me?'

The research took place in three state primary and middle schools in the south-east of England. Participants were, to the best of their knowledge, the only teachers using CDM in their schools. Here is a brief pen picture of each of my participants (pseudonymns are used).

Carl

My first participant, Carl, was in his second year as a qualified teacher working in the primary school where he recently trained. Before entering teaching, Carl studied History and worked in sales and cafés, but 'had it in his head' that he would end up working as a teacher. These experiences as well as captaincy of a football team have some possible bearing on the type of teacher he is today. His focus on History has taught him to take a 'long view' of his pupils' education; his football experience has convinced him of the advantages of teamwork; and his sales experience has perhaps convinced him that

> I'm not going to force ... thirty children to do something they don't want to do – it's a waste of my energy. So you shape it so that they drive it.

Michael

Michael, my second participant, was in his second year of teaching in a middle school, having completed a degree in Primary Teaching. He decided when he was five years old that he wanted to be a teacher. At that age he felt that teachers had 'that kind of celebrity status' and liked the idea of a career around 'learning':

> I've always been a learner. Even now as an adult I still go on learning things in the background while I'm teaching.

He felt very lucky with the education he was given and wanted to give children the same kind of education that he had.

Philip

My third participant, Philip, had been teaching for 17 years at the time of the study. Prior to this, he completed a Sports Science degree and a PGCE and worked as a peripatetic sports coach in schools. He recalled his own schooldays with pleasure. The state primary school Philip attended was run by a non-traditional head teacher who kept animals, believed in children spending time outdoors and did not insist on school uniform. Philip believes that this experience gave him a lifelong interest in animals and ecology. This unorthodox head teacher may also have provided a 'collaboration' role-model for Philip.

Participant 1: Carl

I identified my first participant, Carl, through a discussion we had about one of his pupils, who had been referred to the Educational Psychology Service where I worked. I was involved in a review meeting with Carl a couple of weeks after an initial consultation concerning a socially isolated child, Harry, who was not co-operating in class. I had previously offered some recommendations for Carl to consider, and in our review meeting he told me that he had discussed my recommendations regarding Harry with the whole class, who said they wanted to do it differently. This is the only time in over 30 years that I have come across a teacher independently discussing an EP's recommendations with the whole class. Further discussion suggested that he regularly involved pupils in classroom discussions and decision-making. Shortly after this, he agreed to take part in my research and we met regularly over the next 15 months for in-depth interviews, interspersed with classroom visits.

Carl was the only teacher in that school using CDM. He explained how he had come to use CDM because he wanted to be a nurturing teacher who showed respect to his pupils. This involvement in decision-making seemed to him to be a natural way of doing it: 'As a teacher, you've *got* to treat every child like a person, otherwise you can't *help* them. That's what we're there to *do* ... at the end of the *day*.'

Carl knew that he wanted a classroom where every pupil felt safe and confident to say whatever they wanted, without fear of being ridiculed, or feeling stupid or rejected. So at the start of term they watched lots of YouTube videos together and discussed these as a class, talking about how the people involved might have felt and sharing their own feelings about similar situations. Carl joined in and encouraged children to speak to each other rather than directing their comments to him. He then developed this culture of communication by regularly sharing his plans with them and asking what they thought. If any child appeared to be starting to make a suggestion, or question the way things were done in the classroom, Carl encouraged them to go further. At the same time, he consciously held back from talking himself, encouraging pupils to take a more active role by placing them, rather than himself, centre stage.

Discovering boundaries together

Although Carl was aware that children sometimes say and do inappropriate things, he told the class that they were not going to start with any rules, but to work out the boundaries together as they went along. This led to some interesting discussions, helped the pupils to learn about negotiating relationships and seemed to work, according to Carl.

If children are never given the opportunity in class to collaborate in decision-making, teachers would find it very hard to identify those children who need extra help in this area. Carl realised that in order to develop a collaborative culture in his classroom, with children who had had three to five years of 'being told what to do', some children would need to change perceptions of themselves and others, and would need to learn some new skills. For example, Carl was working with a small group one day when a boy approached needing help. He just stood by the group with his hand up until Carl turned and said, 'With a group this size, you just say, "Excuse me" to get attention.' Carl also recognised that some children did not yet believe that their ideas were valuable enough to express, and he wanted to do something about this.

This example illustrate three points: (1) Carl's belief that every pupil in his class is important; (2) his recognition that some children need nurturing in order to participate fully; (3) and the role the teacher can play in changing both a child's own self-perception, and the way that they are regarded by their peers.

Trust and openness between teachers and pupils are key when developing a collaborative classroom. And Carl's class soon discovered that a difficulty experienced by even one pupil in their class was everybody's business, and something they could all help with. He found ways of involving his class in discussions and support around individual pupils (see Corey's Computer Time later in this chapter) and at the start of term, for example, he asked his class if they would be patient with him while he showed patience to two boys who had not yet 'learnt to be part of the class', which they all accepted and supported.

STORY: SHARKEY

At Parents' Evening, Shaun's mother asked Carl what could be done to help her son to think more highly of himself. Carl told his mum he was going to brainwash him. He said, 'I'm going to make him more confident. I'm going to fix his self-esteem,' and she laughed.

In Carl's school, resilience is represented by a fish; children are encouraged to 'be like a fish' and keep going when things are tough. So for the first six months Carl started calling Shaun 'Sharkey'. He wasn't just a fish, he was a super-fish who was going to learn to be the most resilient person in the school. So he became 'Sharkey' and all the other children started calling him 'Shark', and Carl put a picture of a shark above his desk. He didn't say anything, but Shaun started to be more resilient.

One day the Head came into class to hear the children giving European Union Referendum speeches. Shaun was reluctant to get up. All the other children gathered round him to offer encouragement, urging him on, 'Remember when you couldn't do anything … When you just used to cry … go for it!' Shaun's face filled with pride and he got up and read out his speech.

The head teacher was very complimentary, and Carl was pleased to witness not only Shaun's growing confidence but also the powerful encouragement of the other children and the added affirmation from the head teacher.

As well as putting time by for class discussions, Carl tried to find time to just sit with his pupils to talk about their experiences in and out of school. He knew a lot about them and they knew a lot about him. He tried to make decision-making very much part of the curriculum.

Whilst Carl was providing many more opportunities for pupils to contribute to decision-making, he felt that they needed to know they will not always have this opportunity, and to know how and when to accept or challenge this.

STORY: PLEASE BE PATIENT WITH ME

Carl believed that one of the most important roles of the teacher is to create an inclusive class community. There were some pupils in his new class who, for a range of reasons, had become social 'outliers'. One of these boys had spent the majority of his previous year being taught outside the classroom by a teaching assistant. At the start of term, Carl said to his class, I'd like you all be patient with me while I show patience to two or three boys who have not yet learnt to be part of the class – everybody knows who I'm talking about. There will be times when it might appear as if I'm letting them get away with things that others would get into trouble for, but that's to help them to learn how to be part of the class. After a discussion in which pupils showed that they too wanted a class where everyone felt good about themselves, all the class accepted to be patient and supported Carl wholeheartedly in this endeavour for the rest of the year.

Carl felt he had taken a bit of a risk being so open with the class. But he soon realised that if there was something that he was concerned about regarding the class, that it was not only his business, but theirs also, and that with their co-operation, better and longer-lasting solutions could be found.

Carl made it clear to his class that there are school rules, a National Curriculum and other requirements where there is little room for negotiation. He explained the things that *he* has to do, and stuff *they* have to do, making it clear when external factors, such as school and government policies, are driving decision-making. Whilst encouraging pupils to conform to school expectations he invited them to come up with their own reasons for a rule so that it that makes sense to them. Carl accepted accountability for what was going on in his classroom and whilst he was clear with his pupils that *he* was in charge: 'I set the rules, it's my classroom,' one of his 'rules' was that he was prepared to change things when children questioned them or offered better alternatives. You can read more about Carl in Chapter 6.

Carl was pleased and sometimes amused at the variety of unpredictable ways that his pupils used to take up the shared power he was offering.

STORY: FOX POO CHECK

In winter, there was fox poo all over the playground which was getting on pupils' shoes. Carl decided that when they came in from break one pupil would check shoes. Even if he was five minutes late, the pupils would be standing by the door with their hands up, wanting to be shoe checker. So Carl would open the door to let them in and say, 'Esme, yes you can be shoe-checker.' But one day, the boy picked by Carl to be checker said, 'Could Caroline be shoe-checker?' and she beamed and said, 'Oh yes, thank you,' and she did it. So, without any discussion, the pupils changed the procedure themselves and followed it from that day onwards. Then one day one of the boys told Carl, 'Sir, there isn't any fox poo anymore. Why do we still do this?' Carl said, 'Well that's a very good point. What should we do?' And he said, 'Nothing. Why can't we just line up?' To which Carl replied, 'Okay, that's fine.' Carl was tickled and impressed by that way his pupils had not only used their initiative, but had voluntarily taken up his offer of power-sharing in this imaginative way. What moved and encouraged Carl was that pupils started to choose pupils who either did not generally volunteer or who benefited socially from being chosen.

Carl told me that he was surprised that children didn't only choose their friends, but acknowledged that his efforts to build an inclusive and supportive class community were paying off. His comments on this event reflected his pleasure: 'That's the nicest thing actually. The best thing! But *they* did it; it wasn't me. They did it. I don't even know where it started. They suddenly started saying, "Could someone else be shoe-checker?" It's so nice. It's true, it's good. They're just, oh they're ... it's lovely.'

Carl realised at this point that something in the class culture was changing that enabled children to seek to share the teacher's decision to select pupils for a task. This story made me realise that the power to choose a person to do a task or answer a question is an aspect of teacher authority which could be shared with pupils to good effect. I've since recommended this as an intervention for children who need to be given a legitimate way of meeting the need for power.

This culture of inclusion and helping pupils to be full members of the class is illustrated in Corey's story below.

STORY: COREY'S COMPUTER TIME

Corey was struggling to behave in class and settle down to work, and had become a kind of social 'outlier'. Carl's colleague had previously agreed with Corey and two others that they be rewarded for concentration with extra computer time. Carl told me he felt uneasy with the arrangement, particularly for Corey; he felt it was a ridiculous plan to take an 'unpopular' boy out of the class for half an hour and reward him by moving him away from everybody else.

Carl first talked to these three pupils, explaining why he wanted to adapt the proposal.

Carl: You can't have it every day, because I want you in here practising to be part of the class.

Carl got everybody's attention.

Carl: Look, this is the deal: these three guys have their own reward system ... and they are going to get 15 minutes of computer time each. Is that okay with all of you? Please don't talk, but put your hand up if you've got a problem.

Billy puts his hand up,

Carl: Okay, Billy, what's up?

Billy: I don't think it's fair.

Carl: Why not?

Billy: Because ... they're getting rewarded and we're not.

Carl: Okay, that's fine. But why are they getting rewarded?

Billy couldn't explain it. Carl explained to them that they were getting rewarded because they need the practice.

Carl: I understand they get rewarded for something you guys already do, but they need an incentive to do it. Once they do it comfortably then they won't be rewarded any more.

Billy: (shrugs) Okay, whatever, that's fine.

Carl: Okay. Well what would you like to do? What do you think would be fairer?

Billy: Okay. Well what about if they got to choose someone to go with them?

Carl: Okay, that's fine, we can do that. What happens if they choose the same person every time?

Billy: No. They've got to choose a different person each time.

Carl: That's fine, no problem.

Whilst Billy and Carl were in dialogue, the others in the class were paying close attention, obviously curious and eager to see where this discussion would lead. So the new plan was that these boys could earn 15 minutes computer time each, and would choose one person to take with them. And every week, if they earned the time, they would choose a different person. That meant they were spending 15 minutes eventually with people that they didn't normally speak to.

Carl thought this was a brilliant idea and it fitted perfectly. Because the class had been involved in the decision, the three boys felt supported. With the power to choose a person to share their reward, they didn't need to use other, bothersome, ways of feeling important, and the time spent one-to-one with a classmate helped them to form new bonds.

This story illustrates some of the skills that are useful for CDM:

- an openness to question and amend school approaches, traditions and routines;
- involvement of the whole class in decisions about individual interventions; and
- the use of naturally occurring events as learning for responsible citizenship and community-building.

The above dialogue appears to involve teacher Carl and a single pupil, Billy. However, the scenario described actually involved the whole class, as all the pupils were observing and listening to what is going on, and were learning that:

- the teacher respects them and their views are valuable;
- it is important that all pupils are comfortable with what goes on in their classroom;
- the teacher trusts that they will give their support to Corey and any other pupils who need it;
- their views are taken seriously;
- they don't have to agree with their teacher's proposals – adults don't always have the best ideas;
- talking things out in front of the class is okay;
- the well-being of an individual is community business; and
- decisions about an individual have implications for the class community.

These are valuable lessons for life! Carl is modelling the kinds of skills that we want all pupils to develop not only for the classroom but also for their family and community lives and in their future workplaces.

'It's not fair!'

With rising concerns over adult exploitation of children and young people, training courses on child protection, radicalisation and CSE (child sexual exploitation) are mandatory for professionals, such as EPs, working in the public sector. These courses place an emphasis on how to understand abusive behaviours, and how to identify and support children who may already be subject to exploitation. However, very little is said on courses I have attended about what it is about society that enables a culture of abuse to exist in our communities. Maybe the unchallenged power that some adults hold over children is one of those factors.

The response that Carl made to Billy's comment 'It's not fair', in the example above, shows that it is possible to develop a classroom culture where pupils are not expected to accept without question the opinions, wishes and instructions of adults. Participants' accounts support the idea that when children feel that their opinions and ideas are not only taken seriously, but that they can have an impact on what goes on in their own classrooms, this could contribute to personal resilience and a sense of personal agency. It is likely that these characteristics could be a protective factor against exploitation and radicalisation. It has also been recognised that children can be continually abused, as in the Rotherham case, because nobody listens to them (Lansdown, 2017).

Messy courage

Carl was aware that after even two or three years of schooling, his pupils were already conditioned to expect the teacher to decide everything, and he wanted to address this passivity. So when he could, he would stand back and let the pupils have a go at sorting out any problem situations, rather than diving in and taking over.

This meant that there were times when Carl held back and allowed the class to argue, be distracted and waste time in situations where a more conventional teacher may have intervened to hurry them up, quieten them down, remind, nag, complain and use various methods of control. Carl's plan was that eventually, with no teacher intervention, the children would realise that nothing useful was happening and start to organise themselves. He would then invite them to reflect on what they have been doing, and whether it had got them where they wanted to be. Sometimes this worked, sometimes it didn't. It took a lot of what I call 'messy courage'.

Carl felt that his children had got so used to waiting to be told what to do that they had failed to develop a sense of responsible autonomy. The example of this I saw involved the class moving from the classroom to the hall to play a ball game that they all obviously enjoyed.

STORY: GETTING INTO GROUPS

Carl gave pupils the instruction to go into the hall and form themselves into four teams – something he had asked them to do before, and had supervised. This time, he sat down at the side of the hall and just watched to see what they would do. First of all, they got the balls out and were playing with them until one or two pupils said that they need to get into teams. With some ordering about, arguing and negotiation, they eventually formed into four teams and called Carl over to start the game, by which time some pupils were already grumbling about how much time had been wasted by people not co-operating. They had a great time playing the game, and back in the classroom Carl invited them to reflect on how the groups had been chosen. Some pupils said they wanted Carl to choose the groups because then they could just get on with the game. They decided that they needed to learn how to choose groups, but that for the next lesson, Carl would choose.

Carl was sometimes torn between teaching pupils a rule or routine to follow, and letting them learn this from experience. The pupils frequently spend time simply chatting together as a class in a relaxed and informal way and Carl described how they have some very relaxed times of the day when 'we just sit on the floor and I will just sit back and let them talk'. He sometimes 'backs off' to see if pupils can learn from each other first, aware that whenever he responds first, it is unlikely that another child will have a go at assisting their classmate. He discusses his decisions with the class and asks their input.

Despite the length of time that it was taking for this class to start to take some responsibility for their own behaviour, Carl was patient and had concluded that the more he intervened to sort out class discipline, the less they would do for themselves. He found that lessons such as these, involving discussion and negotiation took a great deal more mental power and had less predictable outcomes than lessons where children simply followed his instructions to the letter. He discovered that it can be exhausting to temporarily feel out of control as a teacher, even when one sets out to 'relinquish control'. In addition, there is an ongoing pressure from colleagues to have a class who just 'gets work done'. However, Carl's tension was reduced by the satisfaction that he was being 'the teacher I want to be' rather than 'the teacher the system wants me to be …. What school wants from the teacher'

Carl acknowledged that teaching children CDM requires more perseverance than teaching them maths, but was determined to continue: 'You wouldn't stop trying to teach someone how to divide, why can't I carry on teaching someone how to make decisions?'

Although he was unaware of it, Carl was often using a recognised approach with his pupils – the Kolb 4-stage learning cycle: he allowed the children to experience what happened without the teacher's control (experience); he gave them the opportunity to reflect on their own behaviours (reflect); they came to some conclusions about what they had been doing (conceptualise); and they came up with ideas for what to do next time (plan).

Obstacles to CDM

Having decided that his classroom was going to be one where children collaborated with their teacher, Carl found that there were many things that got in the way. As he was relatively new to the teaching profession, he was struck by the strong but unspoken expectation of what he described as 'what school wants from the teacher'.

Reflecting on how exhausting it was to allow children to learn from their own decision-making, Carl said he would find the alternative more stressful:

> But, it would be the same, if I was … authoritarian. Except instead of saying, 'Go and make your decision,' I'd be saying, 'You're *in* at break time!'
>
> People *are* going to argue, but learn *how*. Learn how to do *nicely* … then how to resolve your conflicts *yourself*. It should be more *apparent*.

Carl believed that the difficulty his pupils had in managing themselves as a group was not down to immaturity or lack of ability, but rather that they had been de-skilled by three years of teacher-controlled interactions. Whilst Carl's approach did eventually bear fruit, not many teachers would have his patience and confidence in pupils. He was also the only teacher in his school using CDM and whenever he talked about any problems he was having with his class, his colleagues would urge him to start to use more coercion and punishment, which he knew was not the answer. Carl described how he was very much making up CDM as he went along and often felt stuck and unsure what to do next. The lack of a theory contributed uncertainty about using CDM with his class:

> We won't know with this class if they'd had a different teacher they would have come out differently. We'll never know. So I don't know if my way was better or worse.

Positive outcomes identified by Carl

For pupils

- Pupils learn about citizenship through experiencing and discussing social pressures, conformity and collaboration;

- They learn to talk in front of classmates without feeling self-conscious;
- They are learning that:
  - the adult doesn't always have the best ideas;
  - 'talking things out' in front of the class is okay;
  - all pupils have the right to feel comfortable with what goes on in their classroom; and
  - decisions made by, or about an individual may have implications for the whole class.

For Carl

- Eight-year-olds can grasp sophisticated concepts about citizenship, collaboration and social pressure when they are experiencing it themselves;
- Being involved in decision-making is fun for pupils and can lead to learning outcomes the teacher hasn't expected;
- If CDM is not a whole-school approach, pupils need to know that *not every teacher is up for it!*
- Unless CDM is part of a whole-school culture, there is a danger that it is seen by colleagues as simply a personal preference, rather than a recognised way of teaching;
- The whole class can provide valuable assistance when an individual pupil has a problem;
- Naturally occurring events can be used to teach responsible citizenship;
- CDM needs teachers to 'plan loosely so the pupils can shape the lesson';
- CDM involves all pupils, not just those who work hard, or behave well, in having a say in how things are done;
- The teacher has an important role to play in changing a child's negative self-perception and reputation in the class;
- Carl reckoned that many of the problems he experienced using CDM with his class would disappear if this was a whole-school approach; and
- Some children need a lot of teaching, practice, opportunity and encouragement to learn to participate fully in CDM.

Participant 2: Michael

I first identified Michael as a potential participant following a request for EP involvement with a pupil of his. Dean, aged ten, had great difficulty communicating and connecting with people, and was finding his move from first to middle school highly distressing. I was struck by Michael's deep empathy and the unusual lengths to which he had gone get to know this boy and find ways to include him in classroom life. In this consultation, I heard about the way Michael had engaged the class in discussions about helping their classmate and I was impressed by Michael's willingness to adapt his approaches to meet Dean's needs. Following this meeting he accepted an invitation to talk again with a view to participating in my research. Michael gave some examples from his own practice which confirmed that he sometimes shared decision-making with his pupils and valued the concept. I had also heard from his deputy head teacher that Michael's classroom was highly participative. Michael was completing his second year as a qualified teacher when my study started.

Michael's class had developed many 'traditions' that give them the chance to have fun together. As he described to me how they create routines for maintaining classroom order Michael adopted different voices and postures mimicking the children's participation in these scenarios, as though re-living their experience.

STORY: VICTORIAN CLASSROOM

Michael welcomed pupils' suggestions for traditions and routines to overcome the need for constant instructions and reminders. For example, as soon as he put on the James Bond theme, they automatically stopped their maths, put their books away and moved into their places for English. Although this was Michael's initiative, pupils began to suggest their own routines, often related to their Topic. For example, to get order they decided that Michael should say the words 'Victorian classroom!' and they would all sit upright, and in unison, with their best 'queenly' impressions, say, 'We are not amused!' and get back to work with less noise.

In teaching pupils to care for each other, Michael found that they also learned to care for him, and in his second year of teaching he was beginning to realise that there was something he was doing that was creating an ethos he liked, although he was not quite sure what this was.

Michael sees the sharing of details of his life as a kind of partnership with his pupils. 'I was able to turn that into a perseverance thing. And I loved that they were already involved in beforehand because they genuinely cared about me passing. It was really cute.'

Despite Michael's doubts regarding his pupils' abilities to make decisions for themselves, he handed over control to the class more readily when he felt he would not be judged by others on the outcome. His account of the work following a day

STORY: THE DRIVING TEST

The day Michael was taking his driving test his pupils got together and wrote a whiteboard message, 'Good luck Mr Parker' [pseudonym]. They asked the teaching assistant to text him a photograph of the class in front of the whiteboard. She said, 'Just remember that he might not pass, and in that event don't worry because I'm sure the picture will cheer him up'. One of the pupils said, 'He can't fail – he's Mr Parker.' Michael didn't receive the message until late afternoon by which time he'd already failed his test. The next morning he told his class, 'I'm an adult and I failed and that's fine.' He told them that he had already booked his next test, that he would try again and that he would pass.

STORY: THE GOOGLE VISIT

Following a day when some Google employees came in to demonstrate the latest virtual reality technologies, Michael planned for pupils to come back and do some poetry work on it. However: 'when we got back here I said, "Do you know what, actually I've changed my mind I'm not going to tell you what to do." I said, "You're not allowed to do art because we're doing another two hours of art this afternoon, so that's a bit much. But other than that I really don't mind what you do, what you do with what you've just learned about." And I just said, "There's the scrap paper drawer, there is A3 paper, there is A4 paper, there's lined paper. You do what you want with what you've just learned." And their work was brilliant!'

with Google employees illustrates Michael's surprise and joy at the way his pupils made and carried out their plans when he allowed them to decide how they would express their learning from the day.

I asked Michael what was so 'brilliant' about his pupils' work that day, and he said that not only was the co-operation and productivity the best he had ever seen from this class, but that no two children did the same thing; everybody had taken a highly personal approach to exhibiting their learning. What he had not expected was that the children utilised all kinds of information and skills that they had been learning in previous months, demonstrating persuasive arguments and correct punctuation for speech, for example, which they had been studying a couple of weeks earlier. Some pupils who normally produced quite scrappy work were much neater and showed more care in the presentation of the work they produced that day. A few months later I asked Michael whether he had repeated this experience and given pupils more of a free rein in the way they express their learning. He said that he had felt much freer to take this approach after the Google visit, as the pupils' work from this was not going to be assessed. The way he put it was, that he felt more comfortable letting the pupils have more of a say when it 'didn't matter', that is he would not have to be accountable to his managers for the outcomes. Michael told me that the current assessment system discourages teachers from allowing children to make decisions about how they will present their learning, because it is really hard to evaluate and allocate a grade or level to highly original and disparate pieces of work, such as those produced on the Google experience.

At the time of the study, Michael's class had developed a good sense of community and he was continuing to find opportunities to let his class hone their decision-making skills.

Michael discovered for himself some of the concepts that you will come across throughout this book. Once he became more aware of CDM was raised, Michael recognised the dominance of teacher-centred decision-making all around him. He started to revisit previously teacher-led decisions, and invited pupils to participate and was surprised to find that his pupils approached decision-making with a new freshness and energy. Once they perceived that they could be involved in decision-making, pupils started to make suggestions of their own and offer their help in difficult situations. This led him to realise the implications of CDM for the whole school and how radical changes across the school would be needed if he was serious about developing a collaborative culture in his classroom. For example, CDM does not always fit in with existing school 'traditions'.

STORY: STAR OF THE WEEK

Michael told me that following one of our interviews he wanted to try to introduce some CDM into the school's Star of the Week tradition. So he gave each pupil in his form group a slip of paper and said, 'I want you to decide who the star of the week should be. So I want you to vote for someone. But I'd also like you to give a reason, like I do in assembly.'

Michael thought this approach hadn't worked, not because they couldn't do it but because the list of people being voted for was so long. Pupils said, 'I'm going to vote for so-and-so because I know they found this lesson really hard but they tried really well,' or 'I'm going to give it to this person because they've been a really good friend this week,' and things like that; they brought up things that were quite personal to them.

So Michael said to them, 'I can't use this to actually give the Stars of the Week in assembly for two reasons: one because if I gave it to all of you that would be really unfair on the other classes because they only get two. No one has really got a majority vote because you've all been so kind and voted for so many different people. So I'm not going to do that. I'll still do it myself next week but what I will do is I will share all of these with you because they're all lovely.' So he just sat and read them all out. He told me, 'It was really nice. It was quite a nice morale-boosting little five minutes of just things children had said about each other. And I said, "I'm not going to say who has written them but if that person wants to own up to it, then you can do." So they were like, "Yeah that was me." It was quite sweet.'

Positive outcomes identified by Michael

For pupils

- Pupils got themselves into pairs or groups and one or two chose to work on their own;
- All pupils were the most engaged in their work that Michael had ever seen them;
- When pupils were making their own decisions about how to represent their own learning, 'Their work was brilliant.' The work was of a better quality than he had seen before;
- Every pupil's work was individual – no two individuals or groups did the same thing;
- What most surprised and pleased Michael was the way in which they applied recent learning from across the curriculum;
- They respected their access to the class resources and fully co-operated with each other over this; and
- Pupils talked about this lesson for ages afterwards.

For Michael

- Teachers can experience surprise and joy at the way that pupils make and carry out plans when given the freedom to do so.

- At any stage, it is still the teacher's decision to let pupils go ahead with their plans, or to rein them in.
- Aspects of school culture can prevent a teacher from giving pupils opportunities like this. Head teachers need to be aware that teachers need permission and encouragement to have the courage to let go of that control that can inhibit learning.
- Teachers need to be allowed to take risks in their teaching if they are to encourage pupils to take risks in their learning.
- Children can be trusted with resources.

Participant 3: Philip

Philip was introduced to me by an acquaintance of mine, Rob, whose daughter Philip taught. As a governor of the school, Rob remarked that the School Council had flourished with Philip's contributions. When we met, Philip confirmed that he sometimes shared decision-making with his class, and said that he was very interested in taking part in the study as he was responsible for Pupil Voice throughout the school.

Philip's previous experience as a sports coach influenced his teaching style. Philip had been running whole-class philosophy-based sessions for a couple of years, and his pupils were well versed in the procedures of debating philosophical questions. On the training for this approach, Philip had learnt techniques to help children to direct their comments and questions to each other, rather than the teacher. This included adjusting his body position and eye contact so that his pupils did not continually look at him for approval of their comments or questions, even when these were directed towards their peers. When pupils are involved in these philosophy sessions, they learn how to use a range of hand signals to demonstrate and communicate that they are listening, agreeing with the speaker, want to ask a question or make a comment, or have an issue with what is being said. Philip's class became fluent with these hand signals and, without any prompting from him, started using the signals in classroom discussions. The hand gestures had become such a natural way of communicating that pupils seemed unaware that they were starting to bring these gestures into their other class discussions.

It was as a result of being sent on a training course for carrying out this class-based philosophy intervention that Philip started to appreciate the ideas and knowledge that children bring with them into school, that are too frequently underused and unrecognized in conventional classrooms.

Philip felt his present class had responded well to the formal techniques for whole class discussions that their philosophy-based activity involved and was pleasantly surprised when they independently started using some of these for classroom deliberation more generally.

In this account, Philip showed that he valued having a system that overcame some of the common issues of class discussion, such as including less-vocal children. He showed genuine pleasure when describing how pupils started to generalise the hand signals independently in the classroom for other discussions. One thing his pupils found difficult was addressing their comments and questions to each other rather

STORY: PHILOSOPHY SESSIONS

I don't find [the philosophy sessions] threatening, no one is ever kind of *told* that they have to speak. The only thing that I make, that people *do* have to do is they have to show that they're actually *engaging*. If you agree with someone you put your thumbs up, thumbs to the side [*Philip shows me the hand signals*] used by pupils to show they are listening, agree, disagree or want clarification.

So even if they don't want to actually say anything, they can kind of show that they are actually [listening]. It stops children just sitting like this with their hands crossed because that just shows that their actively involved. The teacher doesn't choose who does the speaking, so if you just put your point across about religion and I've got my hand open, then you choose me because I've got my hand open. If I haven't got my hand open you don't ask me.

[In the philosophy sessions] I am called a Facilitator. The child who's just *spoken* chooses the next person, not the adult. The good classes were so well-trained in [this approach] if they wanted to say something they would start putting their hands open just in a normal kind of class situation. And [something] which is *really hard* to do, because children are so trained to speak to *you*, it's actually getting them to not speak to *you* [the teacher]. '*I* don't want to know the answer, I *know* the answer.' it's actually to turn around and tell the class.

than to Philip, their teacher. Their previous five years of teacher-centred classroom decision-making had led them to expect most questions to come from the teacher to the pupils, and for most comments to be directed straight back to the teacher, rather than to each other.

Philip was using CDM to agree ways of improving concentration and behaviour, or in lessons where he had already decided that the outcome could be flexible, and was not subject to formal teacher assessment. He found that most pupils' wishes are easy to fulfil, and some of the things they want a say in did not necessarily make huge demands on the teacher. They also really appreciated having their teacher's decisions explained to them, and being able to have some say about what they learn and how they learn it.

Philip described the open and honest discussions he was able to have this class as 'a real heart-to-heart'. This suggests that it is in these collaborative discussions that a teacher and his pupils connect emotionally. In some brief reflections, Philip summarised the purpose of CDM as being a right; important for a sense of belonging, ownership and self-worth; and pragmatic: if they have decided it, they will make it work.

'It's their school [*Quiet laugh*] … Because actually they've got to come here every day and it's got to be somewhere they *want* to be. And if someone says, if I was being taught by someone and they said, for want of a better word, 'Shut up, your opinion doesn't count,' then I might be pretty much … shut down. Or not want to be here.

'If someone tells you to do something, you feel a bit of an affront don't you? But actually, if they kind of come to their own decisions then they're more likely to do it.

Philip believes that children have a right to question how things are decided in class, and he also sees some of his pupils' *behaviour* as a kind of questioning, especially by pupils who have not yet learned how to 'question' and 'have a say' in an acceptable way. Although he thinks that sometimes pupils question 'the wrong things', he never feels threatened when pupils question the way he does things. He believes that CDM helps children to learn how to communicate using words rather than through their behaviour.

Findings

The interpretation of each participant's data was summarised under four main predetermined 'themes', drawn from the research questions and aims.

How participants shared decision-making with pupils

The examples of CDM employed by participants included design/adaptation of class routines and discussion of and decisions around solutions to classroom problems (relating to behaviour, curriculum, use of time and equipment). No participant was consistently using CDM for any particular situation and there was little CDM around initial curriculum planning and little CDM concerning the physical environment e.g. seating plans or classroom displays.

Where did they get the idea from?

Each participant had his own tale to tell of teachers who had made an impression on him, and these included teachers who had treated pupils as fellow human beings, who gave pupils reasons for doing things and who had generally spent time getting to know pupils as people. All three, despite their frequent frustrations with pupils, held the same 'celebratory perspective of youth' – a generally positive view of children and young people - identified as a characteristic of collaborative teachers (Wilson, 2002).

The meaning that CDM held for participants

Freedom to be ourselves

No participant saw CDM as part of a teacher's role, but as something 'of themselves' that they brought into their practice. The decision to use CDM reflected participants' basic psychological needs (Glasser, 1998) – mainly for Belonging, Freedom and Fun – and aligned with the kind of teacher they want to be.

Michael: Everything in me wanted him to do that … if I could have done that, I would have done it in a heartbeat;

Carl: 'I can't help it. Without that … I wouldn't be who I am';

Philip: We had a real heart-to-heart as a class; 'It's how I *want* to feel'

Michael suggested that the 'fun' he and his pupils get out of CDM might be a good enough reason to keep going. His account of the work following a day with Google employees (see earlier story) illustrates Michael's surprise and joy at the way his pupils made and carried out their plans when he allowed them to decide how they would express their learning from the day.

Children's rights and well-being

In some brief reflections, Philip summarised the purpose of CDM as being a right; important for a sense of belonging, ownership and self-worth; and pragmatic: if they have decided it, they will make it work. All three teachers believe that children have a right to question how things are decided in class.

Participants viewed CDM as instrumental in meeting other objectives: building a sense of community and trust; maintain safety whilst having fun; developing a good relationship with pupils and an orderly classroom.

Barriers and challenges to CDM

School culture

Despite gaining personal and professional satisfaction from CDM, participants found that it was at odds with the need to 'fit in' with institutional norms, and commented on a strong cultural pressure to adopt a 'classroom persona'. Carl and Michael described how, when things were not going well, colleagues' most frequent suggestions were 'impose more sanctions'.

Carl feels that there is an unspoken expectation of '*what school wants from the teacher*' which teachers can fall into without realising:

> 'Teaching becomes mechanical doesn't it? If you put your hand up and say something the teacher says, "Thank you, put your hand down," and picks the next person with their hand up.
>
> I want it to feel more like a conversation that they've always been having, then one comment to the next comment should be in theory a little bit more … *free*, I guess?'

Carl said he feels that lessons involving discussion and negotiation take a great deal more mental power and have less predictable outcomes than lessons where children simply have to follow instructions to the letter, which can become 'soul destroying'. It can be exhausting to feel out of control as a teacher, he added, even when one sets out to 'relinquish control'. This is multiplied by the pressure from colleagues to have a class who just 'gets work done'. He identified a tension between being the teacher he wants to be and 'the teacher the system wants me to be … what school wants from the teacher'. Carl believes that if teachers had more of a say in what goes on in schools and classrooms, that there would be no problem recruiting people to 'this amazing job'.

Participants did not trust their colleagues to nurture any collaborative ethos their pupils had developed. 'You get to September and have to start over again,' with no faith that the next teacher would carry it on. Michael, for one, thinks that 'they'll teach in their *own* way which will probably be more authoritarian'. He recognises that his teaching may be seen as unconventional and imagines that his colleagues sometimes say to themselves, 'What *is* this guy doing?'

Philip recognised that there are some teachers in the school who see it as 'revolutionary' that children can be allowed to get up and walk around the classroom to pick up their own worksheets or be invited to prepare content at home to deliver to classmates in a future lesson – things he says he does frequently.

Philip is also aware that in order to be accepted by other staff, a teacher needs to be seen as 'a team player' and 'your face has to fit'.

Lack of knowledge and skills

Whilst positive feelings about CDM were prompted by pupil responses and participants' own feelings of 'doing what feels right', they were all troubled by a lack of external validation that the way they were relating to their pupils was better for pupils than the more conventional 'teacher decides all' approach. They wondered whether CDM was worth the toll it took on them as teachers.

Carl acknowledged that teaching children CDM requires more perseverance than teaching them maths: 'You wouldn't stop trying to teach someone how to divide, why can't I carry on teaching someone how to make the right choice?'

> People *are* going to argue, but learn *how*. Learn how to do it *nicely* ... then how to resolve your conflicts *yourself*. ... It should be more *apparent*.

The lack of a theory contributes to Carl's uncertainly about using CDM with his class:

> We won't know with this class if they'd had a different teacher they would have come out differently. We'll never know. So I don't know if my way was better or worse.

Michael's big question is:

> Is that better for them, are they going to get a better learning experience from [CDM] and actually is their progress going to be better with me because of the way I'm doing that? Or actually in the long run is it a waste of time because their progress will be the same and actually they're going to go back to someone that's completely different next year anyway.

Children's skills and experience

All three identified that their pupils were not used to CDM: they did not expect it and took a long time to get used to it. They lacked the skills and practice and also lacked the experience of CDM. None of the participants felt that their pupils would have had previous classroom experience of CDM, given the teacher-centric decision-making prevalent in their schools. They recognised that some children were less able than others to participate in CDM and attributed this variously to home background, previous experience with less collaborative teachers, parenting styles, low self-worth and experiences of previous social exclusion in the classroom. CDM appeared, from participants' perspectives, to expose the gap between children from different home backgrounds and uncovered the difficulty some boys in particular had satisfying their need for power in a non-authoritarian classroom, with girls generally being perceived as being more receptive to collaborative practices.

All participants acknowledged that they frequently felt uncertain about how to proceed with CDM. Carl in particular expressed the view that whilst there is a well-trodden path for the authoritarian teacher, there is a lack of exemplars and no theoretical framework available to guide the collaboration-minded professional. Participants were unsure about whether they were 'doing the right thing' and felt a sense of isolation in the absence of a community of collaborative practice with whom to share ideas. They wanted to understand the benefits of CDM for children, how progress might be measured and how to explain CDM to parents and colleagues.

The 'planning dilemma'

All participants acknowledged that when the class decide amongst themselves what approach to take, they are energised and creative and produce their best work ever. However, the direction they take it in is unpredictable, and this is a problem for teachers in a culture where they feel they are required to assess all work on an 'individual pupil' basis, and pupils are expected to complete work in a uniform way. This means that teachers using CDM may have to 'plan for unpredictability' rather than for uniform outcomes.

Teacher voice

Michael felt that teachers today have little 'say' in what and how they teach, so it does not feel natural to offer that 'say' to pupils:

> So if I don't get that as someone with a degree, that's been to 'uni', that knows how to teach children, who has that rapport with them, and can kind of have that vision of where they should be between now and the next seven, eight years, if *I* don't have that [say] how can we give that to a minor?

Philip agrees:

> I think they [senior leaders] listen … they listen but then *they* decide what they're going to do with it.

Interestingly, by the end of the study, Michael had been promoted to Head of Year and started giving his team 'more of a say' in decisions. He also proposed that staff organise their lesson planning as year groups and involve rotating groups of pupils in planning the content and delivery of the curriculum. He wanted to introduce what he described as the 'child's mind's eye within the learning' into lesson planning.

I spoke to Michael when he had been in his new role for a few months. He told me that getting teachers to take part in CDM was even harder than doing it with pupils:

'it was like drawing blood from a stone for a little while. So that was quite difficult as well. It can be almost as hard with adults as it is with *children* [*laughs*]. But, I was very clear with them. I said, 'I'm *not* just going to say this is what we are doing because is not about *me*. It's about us together doing what *we* want to do.' … But it was hard [*laughs*].

In his new role, Michael now had personal experience of the difference that 'having a voice' can make. When I asked him how this felt, he replied:

Exciting, I think, because it's really nice to be able to put my ideas across for the first time … and actually not just be *listened* to but actually come to fruition in some way. I also really like the fact that my confidence in expressing my ideas to the rest of the team is *met* with confidence from them to say 'no'. Which I really like [*laughs*].

Time

With the constant pressure to cover the curriculum, participants felt unable to 'take their time' to develop pupils' abilities to participate in civic decision-making. However, when participants became as engrossed in their pupils' ideas as they themselves were, time ceased to matter; their worries about covering the curriculum were replaced with excitement at the new levels of co-operation, creativity and productivity; uniformity abandoned when imagination was released and exercised. However, Michael reported that he later discovered that they had covered the curriculum in less time than originally planned. Despite this, Michael admitted that he felt judged about how much the class was able to cover each lesson, and was most open to CDM when the outcome 'doesn't matter', that is, when he didn't have to report back to his manager on the outcome of a lesson in the conventional way.

As with other 'initiatives' staff are asked to take on board, Philip saw CDM as just another thing for a busy teacher to remember to do:
But it's just … I mean you know about teachers, it's just like that's another thing I've got to refer to in the classroom.

The pupils

All participants mentioned the difficulty getting children to discuss such issues with each other publically, when they have been conditioned to keep their views to themselves.

Philip: And something which is *really hard* to do, because children are so trained to speak to *you*, it's actually getting them to not speak to *you* [the teacher]. '*I* don't want to know the answer, I *know* the answer.' It's actually to turn around and tell the class.

Philip described how the boys and girls in his class responded differently to the opportunities to discuss issues affecting the class: the girls 'have the skills to do it or the maturity to actually do it. Whereas the boys ... it's an opportunity to kind of ... talk and not do what they're supposed to be doing'.

What supports CDM?

Matching values and beliefs

Maybe the strongest motivator for all three participants was the way in which CDM aligned with their own values and belief systems. They all believed that children need to learn how to get along with others and work out problems together. They found collaboration more productive and satisfying than teachers planning everything and solving every problem by themselves. They also all believed in a fair society, and wanted their classrooms to reflect this.

Being human together

The motivation for participants to continue to share decisions with pupils came most strongly from the feeling of being authentic human beings that CDM gave them and the positive way in which pupils responded over time.

Philip considered that 'It's healthy for children to be able to bounce ideas off each other'. He also saw the freedom of children to be able to express themselves as important:

I like the children to be kind of ... be able to be themselves in the classroom.

Carl considers respect for children as justification for CDM:

As a teacher, you've *got* to treat every child like a person, otherwise you can't *help* them. That's what we're there to *do* ... at the end of the *day*.

Fun

Michael suggested that the 'fun' he and his pupils get out of CDM might be a good enough reason to keep going. His account of the work following a day with Google employees (see earlier story) illustrates Michael's surprise and joy at the way his pupils made and carried out their plans when he allowed them to decide how they would express their learning from the day.

Reduces teacher stress

Having involved the pupils in creating and adapting routines, Michael felt freed from the stress of maintaining order:

And actually since having that, I don't need to tell them anything because it's done. It's enjoyable and it's done.

Philip described a one-off project where he gave the class six topics to research and present to the class. This worked well. One of the unexpected but positive outcomes was that he was relieved of some of his planning: 'that means I didn't have to teach six lessons on those [topics]'.

Reflecting on how exhausting it was to allow children to learn from their own decision-making, Carl said he would find the alternative *more* stressful:

> 'But, it would be the same, if I was ... authoritarian. Except instead of saying, "Go and make your decision," I'd be saying, "You're *in* at break time!"'

Pupils' responses

Perhaps the most motivating factor for participants continuing CDM was the positive response from pupils over time. All three teachers gained a lot of satisfaction from seeing their pupils really enjoying CDM and starting to take on responsibility themselves, rather than passively waiting for their teachers to decide everything for them. Philip found that pupils had fun with CDM and could be good organisers, as long as they had guidance from an adult.

They discovered that pupils were always full of surprises, and when they gave them the opportunity to decide, they often came up with unexpected ideas, utilising all their skills and imagination. Michael was interested to find that, when given the choice, pupils worked in mixed ability groups and worked well together. This surprised him. At those times when given more of a say in how things were done, pupils were highly motivated and did some of their best work. Behaviour was also better when pupils had decided how to work.

When children responded to the opportunities to share in classroom decision-making, it was an intensely satisfying and enjoyable experience for participants, providing unexpected and successful solutions to commonly experienced problems. For Carl, seeing the class ethos becoming more inclusive, enabling 'outliers' to become full members of the class community made it all worthwhile.

Conclusion

Participants' perceptions aligned with previous findings: that shared decision-making can be good for pupils' motivation, community-building, behaviour and well-being. One of the new messages from this research was that there can be similar, and equally important, benefits for teachers themselves. Participants claimed that CDM enabled them to be their authentic selves in the classroom, provided motivating responses from their pupils and ultimately had the potential to reduce workload and stress. At the same time, participants' accounts show that CDM requires patience, skills and knowledge from teachers and pupils alike.

This study identified the need for teachers to have access to authentic examples of CDM and some guidance about what to expect and what to do when hurdles are encountered. When participants struggled to make sense of the range of pupil responses to CDM, and were trying to work out whether their attempts at collaboration were successful or not, they had no theory or models of practice to call upon.

I found that my participants, even though they were already using some CDM with their pupils, had come to accept that they as teachers had no voice in their own school, and were not planning to challenge this. An institutionalised acceptance of nonparticipation and compliance – 'all the decisions are made by other people and we just do as we're told' – is not good for teachers, pupils or the school. In the case of my participants, they were involving their pupils in decision-making *despite* themselves lacking a 'voice' in the school. There is a danger that school cultures can become so hierarchical that even teachers new to the profession do not question the fact that they have little say about how their school is run. This issue of giving teachers a voice has to be taken seriously even if schools are not considering CDM in the classroom as it is such a vital element in teacher well-being and has implications for recruitment and retention of teachers, if what my participants described is true for others.

Participants viewed CDM as instrumental in meeting other objectives, such as Carl's wish to build a sense of communal trust and support between his pupils; Michael's to maintain a safe, low-risk, environment whilst having fun; and Philip's to have a good relationship with his pupils and an orderly classroom. Running through the accounts of my participants was an acceptance of CDM as being their pupils' right and entitlement:

Philip: 'It's their school'
Michael: 'It's their time'

References

Glasser, W. (1998). *Choice theory: A new psychology of personal freedom.* New York, NY: HarperCollins Publishers.

Lansdown, G. (2017). Rotherham: Never Again! … if we listen to children. Retrieved March 13, 2019, from https://www.huffingtonpost.co.uk/gerison-lansdown/rotherham-never-again-if-_b_9366070.html

Rowe, G. (2018) Democracy in the primary classroom. Unpublished thesis. UCL Institute of Education. Retrieved from: www.pupilparticipation.co.uk/resources

Wilson, S. (2002). Student participation and school culture: A secondary school case study. *Australian Journal of Education, 46*(1), 79–102.

2

Rationale and psychology

This chapter is in two sections, addressing the following questions: 'Why collaborate with children and adolescents?' and 'How does CDM work?' In the first section of this chapter I explore the benefits of being clear about your own rationale for CDM and look at the reasons for collaborating with pupils under three headings: Curriculum and learning; Safety and well-being; and Social justice and democracy. In the second section I explore how psychology explains the positive impact that CDM has on motivation, learning, well-being and behaviour.

Why collaborate with children and adolescents?

Traditionally, decisions about curriculum, discipline, use of time and resources, classroom layout and display have been made by teaching staff, not pupils. Teachers are rarely asked to defend or provide evidence for customary practices such as expecting children to remain seated for hours on end, giving spelling homework, or having children put their hands up to answer questions. However, when teachers introduce less conventional approaches they are more likely to be challenged to explain what they are doing and why. When it comes to CDM, which is still rarely offered in our classrooms, it helps to be clear about why you are choosing to listen to your pupils and involve them in classroom decision-making. Such clarity is important as it can help you to:

- Communicate, describe and defend your practices when questioned or challenged;
- Remember what you value about CDM when you are finding it challenging;
- Plan your approach; and
- Assess the impact of CDM.

A key rationale for CDM is that Article 12 of the United Nations Convention on the Rights of the Child makes it a child's *right* to be involved in decisions that affect them (UN General Assembly, 1989). The UK has signed up to this convention and maybe this should be a good enough reason for schools to involve pupils in decision-making. However, given that teachers and school leaders are continually under pressure to justify what they are doing, you might find it useful to consider some of the research which supports CDM.

Curriculum and learning

In a large UK study, Professor Lynn Davies and her team looked at the impact of pupil involvement in collective decision 'with a recognisable social and/or educational outcome' (Davies, Williams, Yamashita, & Ko Man-Hing, 2005). They analysed 75 studies that met this criteria and found a positive link between participation in school decision-making and a range of educational outcomes. These included:

■ Pupils in more collaborative schools were happier and felt more in control of their learning;

■ Participation enhanced skills of communication and competence as a learner; and

■ Skills in specific curriculum areas improved.

Pupils who experienced greater participation also showed greater self-esteem and confidence. Teachers also reported that when pupils gave them feedback on their teaching, it improved their practice and gave pupils greater insight into the learning process. The researchers attributed this to pupils being trusted with responsibility and the consequent ownership they felt for decisions they helped to make regarding their schools. Davies suggested that those pupils who participated in school decision-making became more skilled in interpersonal communication, including listening to the views of others. Pupils also became more engaged in learning and developed a greater belief in themselves. This was particularly true for those with special educational needs. It was notable that none of the 75 secondary schools in the study showed any evidence that they had reverted to less collaborative practices. Indeed, all reports suggested that pupil participation in decision-making had noticeable benefits, not only for pupils themselves, but for the school and community.

Similar results have been reported for studies in primary schools. For example, Chris Brough studied three teachers who were using 'student-centred curriculum integration' – a term used by the New Zealand government to denote a negotiated process similar to CDM. Brough found that by gradually introducing more and more collaboration and negotiation with pupils, the teachers gained in confidence with using this approach, and pupils responded with better engagement, improved oral and problem-solving skills and were able to apply their learning across wider contexts. Additionally, pupil–teacher relationships improved, and pupils who had previously held back from contributing verbally to lessons found their voice (Brough, 2012).

In my own study (Rowe, 2018), participants felt that in generating and discussing options as a community, their pupils were also acquiring useful skills for future family, work and community collaboration. Carl, my first participant, also found that through learning how to share their ideas, appreciate other people's point of view and challenge the status quo, pupils became better at 'arguing' – a recognised academic and life skill (Andrews, 2009).

A relevant curriculum

For pupils to be more engaged and motivated, the curriculum has to be relevant to their lives, connecting with their interests and experiences, and when pupils believe they have an influence about what happens in the classroom, this significantly improves their educational achievement. As they become more involved in the deliberation, planning and design of what goes on in their classrooms, pupils learn about what it takes to plan a task, organise a classroom or lead a project. Teachers are able to use pupils' wishes and needs to plan and adapt a higher-quality, more appropriate curriculum. When these discussions involve *ways* of learning, this can lead to higher-order thinking skills, enabling pupils to acquire a 'technical language' to talk about learning (Rudduck & Flutter, 2000). Teachers tell me that they enjoy being active responders to pupils' enquiries – as opposed to task-setters – and classroom and school decisions made in cooperation with pupils tend to have better outcomes. As you will gather from several stories in this book, when pupils choose it, they do it.

If we want to know what pupils are thinking about the way we do things, we need to ask them. When we listen, we get to learn things we wouldn't otherwise know, and so decisions made in collaboration with pupils are generally better informed (Boomer, 1992). A teacher once told me that she asked pupils for feedback after every lesson. In the knowledge that all children leave a lesson feeling good, bad or neutral about the experience, she wanted to know which of these it was. Knowing about children's concerns meant that she could address them before they escalated. She was clear that becoming a better teacher started with listening to those who were most affected by her teaching – the pupils themselves. Other teachers who have been involved in action research on pupil consultation also report that their own professional practices improved when pupils are able to give them feedback (Arnot, McIntyre, Pedder, & Reay, 2004). For some, this can even result in a 'renewed excitement about teaching' (Rudduck et al., 2003). Who wouldn't want that?

There is little doubt that pupils feel more in control of their learning if they believe they are making real decisions about it (Glasser, 1997). Children feel happy when they are learning something that they have chosen themselves, and when they succeed, particularly when this has required effort and persistence, they feel good about themselves – if the lesson plan was theirs, they are going to put everything into making it a success. They also feel good about those teachers with whom they associate this satisfying experience.

Two things that pupils tell me gets in the way of them being happy in their learning are stress and boredom; stress when the demands placed on them are too high and boredom when they are too low. It makes sense that the best way to ensure that the level of demand placed on the class is neither too high or too low is to involve the pupils in the design of their own curriculum.

Safety and well-being

When we hear about children being recruited into terrorism and criminal and paedophile rings, it can feel there is really nothing we can do about this in school. On the other hand, how can children resist the criminal grooming of malevolent adults after years of being told that adults are always right? If children are told through school that they must never question an adult's instruction, nor speak up when they feel they've been unjustly treated, how can they be expected to respond when they are asked to do something that feels uncomfortable or wrong?

The child protection and safeguarding training I regularly receive informs me that adults groom children by developing a relationship with them which is based on children being made to feel important, wanted and valued. Maybe children whose views are taken seriously in school, who are encouraged to stand up for themselves and trust their own judgements, are less vulnerable to exploitation? Given the increasing danger of internet and social-media grooming, it is more important than ever that children are given a sense of worth in their own classrooms. CDM gives them the opportunity to have an impact and feel their views are important and worth listening to, and research suggests that such engagement makes it less likely that individuals will be attracted to risky and irresponsible behaviour later on (Public Health England, 2014). Children and adolescents need to know that their feelings and opinions really matter, and be able to express these and believe they have a right to be involved in decision-making. This is unlikely to happen in classrooms where pupils are expected to accept without question the opinions, wishes and instructions of adults.

Although not all teachers will knowingly come across children who are subjects of exploitation, nearly all teachers will have some experience of pupils identified with some level of mental health concern. The World Health Organisation recognises that giving children training in, and opportunities to practice, life skills such as decision-making, assertiveness and interpersonal communication is crucial to maintaining and restoring good mental health (Marmot & Bell, 2012).

As well as being good for children and adolescents, teachers in my study suggested that CDM is also good for adults. Although CDM requires teachers to develop some new skills and for the school to undergo important organisational changes, CDM has been shown to reduce teacher stress and workload, and can lead to greater job satisfaction and improved relationships with pupils. Although it sounds counterintuitive, it does appear that when teachers choose to share power they worry less about losing it, and gain more control rather than less. It appears that the more power teachers hang onto, the more energy they need to maintain it.

It is likely that those teachers whose own psychological needs are met are in the best position to look after the needs of pupils (I look at this in more detail in the psychology section). Recent studies on well-being in the workplace emphasise the importance of workers being in control of their own workload and being involved in decisions about how they carry out their work (Farmer & Stevenson, 2017; Kelchtermans, 2006). This suggests that in the same way that collaborative decision-making is needed for children's well-being, teachers need this just as much for themselves.

Workload is frequently cited as a source of teacher stress. Although it takes time and skill to develop a collaborative classroom, teachers in my study claimed that CDM actually saved them time. When pupils are involved in planning the curriculum, they put in a lot of their own time to seek out information, plan activities and prepare presentations, meaning that teachers don't have to do these things themselves. Once pupils are invited to offer their own ideas and services for the benefit of the class, teachers are freed up to do those many things that pupils can't do themselves.

Highly successful Indian business leader Vineet Nayar has a management philosophy tagged 'Employee First, Customer Second' (Nayar, 2010). The logic behind this philosophy is that in a service industry, employees are the product that his customers are buying. If you think about how Nayar's philosophy relates to the management of schools, it becomes clear that Head Teachers and Senior Management Teams need to create systems and methodologies to nurture teachers and allow them to create more value than anybody else can create.

Who creates the value for the pupil? Who does the pupil want to deal with? Who is the organization for the pupil? The teachers! What kind of school does a pupil want to be in? The one where the teachers feel highly valued! In Chapter 7 we will look more closely at what head teachers can do about this.

Social justice and democracy

A recent collaboration between the UCL Institute of Education and other universities in Europe and the US emphasised that the most effective educational mechanisms for reducing inequality are those which enable individuals to maintain a sense of control over their lives, learn how to tackle major life decisions and take an active stance in civic engagement (Schoon & Silbereisen, 2017). One of the research papers contributing to this study described how young people's 'civic engagement' (that is, voluntary activity that is 'collective' and 'addresses issues of public concern') is an important factor for a successful transition to adulthood (Flanagan & Levine, 2010). They indicate that this civic engagement is largely shaped in the school years and explain why it is so important for democratic societies: communities need people who care about social issues and know how to put ideas into action; children and young people benefit socially and emotionally from civic engagement; and such engagement makes it less likely that individuals will be attracted to risky and irresponsible behaviour later on. Such findings further reinforce the importance of shared decision-making in the classroom.

Some children start school already able to communicate their opinions and wishes in a way that gets a positive response from their teachers. Others have not yet learnt how to do this and may either keep their views to themselves or find that their rudimentary attempts to 'have a say', often expressed through their behaviour, just get them into trouble. For example, a child may rip up her neighbour's work because she didn't understand how to do the task herself but doesn't know how to get help. When children are unable to communicate what they want, without fear, they can feel as though they have no control over what happens to them. Feelings of powerlessness are at the root of many school and social problems.

Concern has been raised about the way in which some inner city schools are setting out to develop a strongly authoritarian 'no excuses' school culture, in the face of research suggesting that this approach can harm children from poor families. These schools, it is claimed, develop 'worker learners' who are discouraged from questioning or challenging their teachers and who hold back their opinions, learning to defer to authority figures; none of which encourage aspirational thinking (Ferguson, 2017; Golann, 2015; The Sutton Trust, 2019). A large-scale study into effective classroom pedagogy in primary education (EPPE) found that there was a cluster of teacher behaviours that benefitted the most disadvantaged children. Amongst this list of behaviours was the *avoidance* of 'over control' and 'the willingness by teachers to share the locus of control and authority' (Siraj & Taggart, 2014). It does seem that teaching approaches that give pupils more control over their learning are *particularly* powerful for those from disadvantaged backgrounds. However, research shows that these children, who have the greatest need for shared decision-making (CDM), are the least likely to experience it in schools where the main opportunities for CDM are in extracurricular activities, and so the benefits of CDM and well-being are particularly strong for these children (Cullinane & Montacute, 2017; The Sutton Trust, 2015).

In an era where democracy as a vehicle for peace and sustainability is of worldwide interest (see e.g., Law & Miura, 2015), it makes sense that children need to learn to understand and value it. In order to learn about democracy, children need opportunities to learn how to take part in civic decision-making. With the many decisions that are made during the day, week, term and year in classrooms and schools, there must surely be room for some of these decisions to be made in collaboration with pupils? For many children, school is the main place that they learn to interact with people outside their own family and so the classroom is good place to learn how to get along with others in a community containing people who have different backgrounds, interests and experiences to themselves. The experience of being listened to, and hearing the views and perspectives of others, helps pupils to respect differences, leading to greater tolerance and understanding of others' needs.

As well as having benefits for the individual, CDM can also benefit the school and wider community.

Potential outcomes for the school:

- Improved teacher–pupil relationships.
- Better attendance (National Educational Board Leasa Oideachais, 2008).
- Less conflict, more cooperation.
- Increased motivation and engagement leads to improved educational attainment (Davies et al., 2005).
- Greater inclusion and sharing of social responsibility for class' and school's social cohesion (Colbert & Arboleda, 2016; Dürr, 2004)
- A climate of trust, understanding and acceptance (Cook-Sather, 2002; Fraser, 2012).
- Pupils and teachers feel free to use their creativity to contribute to school ventures (Bahou, 2011; Leitch et al., 2006).
- Feeling involved and valued, individuals are more likely to be more pro-school (Riley & Docking, 2004).
- Pupils are more likely to respect and support behaviour strategies if they believe that fellow pupils helped to construct them (Bjorklund & Rehling, 2010)

Potential outcomes for the community:

- A future community-focused and politically aware generation, skilled in negotiation and decision-making (Forero-Pineda, Escobarrodriguez, & Molina, 2006; Yamashita, Davies, & Williams, 2010).

- Better communication between the generations (Cooperrider, 1996).
- An increased sense of agency makes it more likely that pupils will volunteer and take part in community ventures (Bahou, 2011; Fielding, 2012).

How does CDM work?

In this section, I explore how psychology explains the positive impact that CDM has on motivation, learning, well-being and behaviour.

When teachers, such as those in my study, create a class ethos where people share experiences and feelings without fear of ridicule or failure, something happens to pupils:

- The distinction between pupils and their teachers starts to become blurred; instead of seeing each other in distinct and power-defined roles, they are working together as fellow human beings;
- Pupils start to value the views of others;
- They learn that their own views count and that they can really make a difference;
- Pupils start talking about things they know a lot about: their own lives, interests and feelings;
- Children who didn't previously contribute during classroom discussions, unsure that their facts are correct, start to have a voice (Rowe, 2018).

It appears that CDM starts off a process that leads to other, linked, benefits: pupils see school as a place where they feel important and worthwhile; their attendance improves; they connect better with their teachers and have less conflict with them; and this improved engagement and motivation has a knock-on effect on their educational achievement. My research participants helped me to see that CDM can offer a similar positive chain of events for teachers:

- They find out more about the pupils' skills and interests, often seeing pupils in a new way with raised expectations;
- They no longer feel the need to come up with solutions to every classroom problem on their own;
- Implementing feedback from pupils around curriculum design results in better teaching;
- Conflict is reduced with previously challenging pupils;
- Teachers feel more in control of the classroom culture, as they have purposefully designed it to be collaborative, rather than leaving it to chance;
- They see how learning improves, bringing higher job satisfaction;
- Two of the participants in my research suggested that CDM may even have implications for teacher recruitment and retention;
- CDM can be fun for teachers too.

How do these changes come about? There are many theories in psychology that might explain why CDM contributes to some of the outcomes described in the first part of this chapter. I have chosen to focus on just three of these – Choice Theory, the Stages of Moral Development, and the Theory of Planned Behaviour – as they cover a range of aspects of human behaviour and motivation which are relevant to the teaching situation. I will also comment on research linking CDM to brain activity, and on a psychological technique known as 'priming'.

Choice Theory

The Psychiatrist Dr William Glasser developed Choice Theory, which proposes that every human being has five basic genetic needs which drive all behaviour: love and belonging; power and self-worth; freedom; fun; and survival (Glasser, 1998). Choice Theory states that the human system continually strives to be in a state of both physical and psychological homeostasis. That is, the human system has a preferred state, and when it is out of balance our creative system is mobilised to try to get us back into a balanced state. This has been long accepted for our physical survival needs, but is now also accepted as true of our psychological needs. Just as our creative system responds to the sensory trigger of thirst, motivating us to seek a drink when the sodium levels in our system are out of balance, so too we are motivated to act when we perceive that our psychological needs are out of balance. For example, an individual who is feeling neglected or rejected seeks to satisfy that need by seeking connection with others.

Before I describe how CDM and Choice Theory are linked, I will give a fuller description of these five needs:

Love and belonging – being valued and wanted by others around you; feeling part of a team, family or community. Belonging is arguably the most powerful of the psychological needs, and one that if a pupil is having difficulty satisfying will dominate their behaviour as they attempt to meet it.

Power and self-worth – feeling capable, competent and valuable; being able to make a difference; having your worth recognised.

Freedom/autonomy – being able to control your environment and work in a way that feels valuable; free from fear, threats and coercion.

Fun and enjoyment – feeling good about the activities themselves, rather than just doing them for a secondary gain such as pay, exam results or to please another person.

Survival – the satisfaction of basic physical needs (including shelter, physical comfort, nutrition, sleep and sex).

Why do these needs matter? When pupils find it difficult to meet their needs in the school setting, these needs do not go away. Instead, they create behaviours in the individual to help them to find ways to meet that need. For example, pupils who do not feel free to express themselves in school, and are not able to be in the driving seat of their own learning, find other, less welcome ways to meet their need for freedom, such as occupying themselves with activities of their own choice; arguing with teachers; or fidgeting, chatting and moving around in lessons. When the skills and capabilities of pupils are not being fully used, they are not meeting their need for enjoyment. This leads to boredom and passivity and sometimes disruption. Pupils may look around and see that there are no legitimate ways to meet this need and so resign themselves to a passive role in the classroom. Others who are less patient may get into trouble for devising alternative classroom activities for their own amusement. Pupils quickly learn to keep their opinions to themselves and to sit and wait for the teacher to decide everything for them. Conversely, in a school environment that enables pupils to meet all of these basic needs, the individual's creative system is freed up for learning, instead of being engaged in finding ways to satisfy these needs. It might help to envisage the impact that an unmet physical need has on our behaviour: for example, if someone starts up a conversation when I am standing in the freezing cold rain with no shelter. My homeostatic system signals to me to move into a more comfortable place, and until I do, this system is unlikely to allow me to concentrate fully on the conversation.

Each one of the five basic needs is important, and there are a number of ways that CDM creates a needs-satisfying classroom and school. When we perceive a goal to be needs-satisfying, we are more likely to put energy into it, and offer our co-operation.

Kohlberg's Stages of Moral Development

Lawrence Kohlberg's Stages of Moral Development goes some way to explaining why decision-making in partnership with teachers and other helps children to develop higher moral reasoning; put simply, 'deciding between right and wrong'. This theory proposes that when someone discusses moral issues with others who are already at a higher level of moral development, they will shift towards that upper level. This shift will only happen if there is some closeness or feeling of similarity with the other person. Kohlberg challenged teachers to create collaborative classrooms where teachers and pupils could engage in intergenerational learning to facilitate this moral shift (Power, 2013).

A word of warning: CDM can have negative repercussions if used as a means of control or manipulation. Although there are reports of participation playing a role in improving attendance or engagement in lessons, if pupils think that they are only being asked to get involved in decision-making as a way to get them to work harder or fulfil a school's goals, any trust, influence and goodwill that might have been developed will be reversed. There is evidence that perceptions are most difficult to shift when the motivation for making that shift is linked to external control (Ryan & Deci, 2000). That is, pupils who feel pressured to change their point of view are less likely to do this than if they feel they have made this choice of their own free will.

Theory of Planned Behaviour

The Theory of Planned Behaviour (TPB) was devised by Social Psychologist Icek Ajzen in the 1980s. TPB describes the factors that affect the probability that an individual will engage in given behaviour (Ajzen, 1991). This theory helps to explain why pupils are more likely to engage and stick to decisions that they have contributed to. TPB states the likelihood of an individual engaging in a given behaviour is increased if they:

■ value that behaviour;
■ believe that their peers, or others they identify with or admire, approve of that behaviour; and
■ believe that the behaviour is under their control.

It follows that when a class decision is made collaboratively, pupils see their peers supporting and contributing the decision. Because they have contributed to it they are more likely to value it. Given that pupils are more likely to suggest actions that they believe are in their control, this theory suggests that motivation and engagement will follow.

Running through all these theories is a psychological concept described as 'agency', which is the ability to control what happens to us; of being able to have part in deciding one's future. A 'sense of agency' is the perception that we can influence our own future and are not just victims of fate or of other people's decision-making. The presence or absence of this sense of agency can really influence the way we feel about ourselves, our learning and social relationships. Would you rather have pupils who felt disengaged and powerless or pupils who want to play a part in their own education and future?

Impact of CDM on the brain

Neuroscientists have found that when people have a sense of belonging and feel that their views have status, this actually impacts *on the brain*. The human nervous system responds differently depending on how much control we believe we have over what happens to us, working best when we feel in control. It appears that we humans are naturally disposed to participate in decision-making.

For example, the pre-frontal cortex plays a key role in the development of executive functions, which include reasoning, concentration, planning and persistence. Professor of Neuroscience Adele Diamond and her team have discovered that this part of the brain operates most effectively when we feel worthwhile, acccepted and actively involved in our learning. They conclude that it may be the case that:

> 'being a member of a cohesive group working toward the important shared goal of helping one's community or helping to make the world a better place … could improve children's thinking skills and the same time bring them joy, increased self-confidence, improved fitness, and a social support group.'
>
> (Diamond, 2014)

It appears that humans are naturally disposed to participate in decision-making, and that feelings of being a powerful person can have positive effects on the working of the nervous system. This suggests that participation in CDM could contribute to development of a child's reasoning and confidence. Diamond also notes that children from disadvantaged homes benefit the most from attempts to ensure that their views have status.

In psychology, 'executive functioning' is the term used to describe the mental processes of remembering, paying attention, planning, organising information and regulating behaviour in order to complete a task or meet a goal. Executive functions (EFs) are needed to help social development (working out how to interact with other people and remember their names, for example), and are themselves affected by social experiences (if children have been previously rejected by peers or a teacher it can affect their classroom concentration and memory, for example). Diamond and her colleagues propose that the best approaches to improving EFs and school outcomes will probably be those that (1) engage pupils' passionate interests, bringing them joy and pride; (2) address stresses in pupils' lives, attempting to resolve external causes and to strengthen calmer, healthier responses; (3) have pupils vigorously exercise; and (4) give pupils a sense of belonging and social acceptance (Diamond & Lee, 2011). All of these are highly consistent with CDM.

Priming

In psychology there is a concept called 'priming', which happens when we expose an individual to one stimulus with the intention of affecting how they will respond to a later stimulus. Priming is used in educational programmes where the state of the learner is crucial to the success of the tasks that follow. For example, pupils can be primed to feel confident to tackle new information, by being given familiar texts to read that they have read successfully in a previous lesson. It is worth thinking about the priming effect of CDM on the brain. At the start of lessons planned by the teacher, the teacher is the only person in the room who has prior knowledge of the lesson content and process – after all, they designed it. However, one of the reasons why pupils quickly engage in a lesson they have been involved in planning is that the experience of anticipating a lesson they have planned themselves acts as a form of priming – they arrive at the lesson 'tuned to the right channel', as it were.

In a conventional classroom, the teacher knows before a lesson starts what the plan is: the learning outcomes; the content to be covered; the tasks to be completed; the materials and resources that are to be made available; and the time that will be allocated to each task. The pupils are dependent on the teacher's decision-making in all these areas and have to wait for the teacher to tell them what to do, how to do it and how long to take.

Researchers set up an experiment to see whether priming – in this case, exposure to learning materials prior to an educational task – would affect pupils' behaviour and academic performance (Koegel, Koegel, Frea, & Green-Hopkins, 2003). The priming consisted of familiarising the pupils with the materials for the next day's lesson in a 'relaxed, non-demanding manner'. It didn't matter if the pupil didn't understand the materials, it was familiarity that mattered. The impact of this simple priming was a decrease in problem behaviours and better engagement and cooperation with the academic tasks in the actual lesson. Although this research was carried out with pupils with a diagnosis of autism, other research supports the priming effect on academic engagement more generally.

This suggests that CDM involving pupils in curriculum design can have a positive priming effect explaining some of the improved engagement, co-operation and productivity associated with CDM.

References

Ajzen, I. (1991). The theory of planned behavior. *Organizational Behavior and Human Decision Processes, 50*, 179–211.

Andrews, R. (2009). *The importance of argument in education. Inaugural lecture.* Institute of Education, University of London. Retrieved from http://citeseerx.ist.psu.edu/viewdoc/download?doi=10.1.1.465.7159&rep=rep1&type=pdf

Arnot, M., McIntyre, D., Pedder, D., & Reay, D. (2004). *Consultation in the classroom.* Cambridge: Pearson Publishing.

Bahou, L. (2011). Rethinking the challenges and possibilities of student voice and agency. Educate~ *The Journal of Doctoral Research in Education Kaleidoscope. Special Issue* 2011 (January), 2–14. Retrieved from http://www.educatejournal.org/index.php/educate/issue/archive

Bjorklund, W. L., & Rehling, D. L. (2010). Student perceptions of classroom incivility. *College Teaching, 58*(1), 15–18.

Boomer, G. (1992). Negotiating the curriculum. *In negotiating the curriculum: Educating for the 21st century* (pp. 4–14).

Brough, C. J. (2012). Implementing the democratic principles and practices of student-centred curriculum integration in primary schools. *Curriculum Journal, 23*(3), 345–369.

Colbert, V., & Arboleda, J. (2016). Bringing a student-centered participatory pedagogy to scale in Colombia. *Journal of Educational Change, 17*(4), 385–410.

Cook-Sather, A. (2002). Authorizing students' perspectives: Toward trust, dialogue, and change in education. *Educational Researcher, 31*(4), 3–14.

Cooperrider, D. L. (1996). The "child" as agent of inquiry. *Organization Development* ..., 1–4. Retrieved from http://appreciativeinquiry.case.edu/ai/uploads/Child_As_Agent.pdf

Cullinane, C., & Montacute, R. (2017). *Life Lessons: Improving essential life skills for young people.* London: The Sutton Trust & Education Endowment Foundation [EEF].

Davies, L., Williams, C., Yamashita, H., & Ko Man-Hing, A. (2005). *Inspiring schools impact and outcomes – Taking up the challenge of pupils' participation.* London: Esmee Fairbairn Foundation with Carnegie UK Trust.

Diamond, A. (2014). Want to optimize executive functions and academic outcomes? Simple, just nourish the human spirit. In P. D. Zelazo & M. Sera (Eds.), *Minnesota Symposia on Child Psychology – Developing cognitive control processes: Mechanisms, implications and interventions* (Vol. 37, pp. 205–230). Hoboken, NJ: Wiley.

Diamond, A., & Lee, K. (2011). Interventions shown to aid executive function development in children 4 to 12 Years Old. *Science,* (New York, N.Y.), *333*(6045), 959–964

Dürr, K.H. (2004). *The school: A democratic learning community. The All-European Study on Pupils' Participation in School.* Strasbourg: Council of Europe.

Farmer, P., & Stevenson, D. (2017). *Thriving at Work: The Independent Review of Mental Health and Employers.* London.

Ferguson, D. (2017). Working-class children get less of everything in education - including respect. *The Guardian.* Retrieved from https://www.theguardian.com/education/2017/nov/21/english-class-system-shaped-in-schools

Fielding, M. (2012). Education as if people matter: John Macmurray, community and the struggle for democracy. *Oxford Review of Education, 38*(6), 675–692.

Flanagan, C., & Levine, P. (2010). Civic engagement and the transition to adulthood. *The Future of Children, 20*, 159–179.

Forero-Pineda, C., Escobarrodriguez, D., & Molina, D. (2006). Escuela Nueva's impact on the peaceful social interaction of children in Colombia. In A. W. Little (ed.), *Education for all and multigrade teaching: Challenges and opportunities* (pp. 256–300). Netherlands: Springer.

Fraser, B. J. (2012). *Classroom Environment.* Routledge Library Editions: Education. https://doi.org/doi:10.4324/9780203125885

Glasser, W. (1997). A new look at school failure and school success. *Phi Delta Kappa*, *78*(8), 596–602.

Glasser, W. (1998). *Choice Theory: A new psychology of personal freedom.* New York: HarperCollins Publishers.

Golann, J. W. (2015). The paradox of success at a no-excuses school. *Sociology of Education*, *88*(2), 103–119.

Kelchtermans, G. (2006). Teacher collaboration and collegiality as workplace conditions. A review. *Zeitschrift Fur Padagogik*, *52*(2), 220–237.

Koegel, L. K., Koegel, R. L., Frea, W., & Green-Hopkins, I. (2003). Priming as a method of coordinating educational services for students with Autism. *Language, Speech, and Hearing Services in Schools*, *34*(3), 228–235

Law, E., & Miura, U. (2015). *Transforming teaching and learning in Asia and the Pacific: Case studies from seven countries.* Paris: UNESCO.

Leitch, R., Gardner, J., Mitchell, S., Lundy, L., Clough, P., Galanouli, D., & Odena, O. (2006). *Researching Creatively with Pupils in Assessment for Learning (AfL) Classrooms on Experiences of Participation and Consultation. TLRP Research* Briefing, 36. London: TLRP.

Marmot, M., & Bell, R. (2012). Fair society, healthy lives: strategic review of health inequalities in England post-2010. *Public Health*, *126*, *Suppl*, S4–10.

National Educational Board Leasa Oideachais. (2008). *School Attendance and Participation : What Works and Why ?*

Nayar, V. (2010). *Employees first, customers second: Turning conventional management upside down.* Boston, MA: Harvard Business School Publishing.

Power, F. C. (2013). Lawrence Kohlberg (1927–1987) – Stages of Moral Judgment, Moral Education.

Public Health England. (2014). *The link between pupil health and wellbeing and attainment.* London.

Riley, K., & Docking, J. (2004). Voices of disaffected pupils: Implications for policy and practice. *British Journal of Educational Studies*, *52*(2), 166–179.

Rowe, G. (2018) Democracy in the primary classroom. Unpublished thesis. UCL Institute of Education. Retrieved from: www.pupilparticipation.co.uk/resources

Rudduck, J., Arnot, M., Fielding, M., MacBeath, J., Myers, K., & Reay, D. (2003). Consulting pupils about teaching and learning. Cambridge: Teaching and Learning Research Programme [TLRP]. Retrieved fromhttp://oer.educ.cam.ac.uk/w/images/6/63/Student_voice-1.pdf

Rudduck, J., & Flutter, J. (2000). Pupil participation and pupil perspective: carving a new order of experience. *Cambridge Journal of Education*, *30*(1), 75–89. https://doi.org/10.1080/03057640050005780

Ryan, R. M., & Deci, E. L. (2000). Self-determination theory and the facilitation of intrinsic motivation, social development, and well-being. *American Psychologist*, *55*(1), 68–78.

Schoon, I., & Silbereisen, R. (Eds.). (2017). *Pathways to adulthood: Educational opportunities, academic motivation and attainment in times of social change.* London: UCL IOE Press.

Siraj, I., & Taggart, B. (2014). *Exploring effective pedagogy in primary schools: Evidence from research.* London: Pearson.

The Sutton Trust. (2015). *The pupil premium: Next steps.* London: Education Endowment Foundation.

The Sutton Trust. (2019). *Elitist Britain.* London: The Sutton Trust with The Social Mobility Commission.

UN General Assembly. (1989). Convention on the Rights of the Child.

Yamashita, H., Davies, L., & Williams, C. (2010). Assessing the benefits of students' participation. In S. Cox, C. Robinson-Pant, C. Dyer, & M. Schweisfurth (Eds.), *Children as decision makers in education.* London: Continuum.

3

Monitoring and evaluation

The three participants in my study felt CDM was working for them some of the time, but at other times they really wondered whether it was worth the effort (Rowe, 2018). At these times, they wondered whether CDM was better than the alternative and whether their pupils would be better off or worse off as a result of collaboration. The evidence they were using to make judgements of the effectiveness of their approach were generally qualitative and subjective: how they, as teachers, felt about using CDM and how their pupils were responding. Although none of my three participants are expected to set communal objectives for their classes, they all had ideas in their heads for how they wanted their pupils to be as a class, which they may have articulated for the first time through the research interviews. Of the three, Carl probably expressed these objectives most specifically:

- Inclusion: to reintegrate the 'outliers' back into the classroom (see Carl's story: Be patient with me);
- Discipline: the class to be able to self-regulate noise levels and form themselves into groups independently of the teacher (see Carl's Shushing Story); and
- Engagement: for all pupils to feel safe to express themselves in the classroom and to be able to offer suggestions about the curriculum.

In Chapter 2, I stressed the importance of having a clear rationale to make it easier to evaluate impact. I want to say a bit more about that now. I suggest that if you are carrying out an evaluation of the impact of *collaboration*, this is best done in collaboration with pupils. The following steps may be helpful:

1. Select rationale: be clear about your own rationale for using CDM (e.g., we want our class to feel like a community and support each other in their learning. We want improved co-operation and productivity).

2. Community objectives: discuss the principles of CDM with your pupils: 'I want to you to help me make some of the decisions that I usually make without you ...' and ask them what difference they think this would be make. List these. Maybe use an outcome wheel similar to the Corporate Steering Wheel

(Marr, 2020), used by Tesco, to encourage pupils to consider what matters to them, and also consider outcomes they may not have thought of themselves. You could then create your own class steering wheel with class-specific outcomes. Your class steering wheel might have an agreed class title, logo, mascot or motto as its hub, with agreed objectives around the rim. This could be adapted for secondary school subject specialists or primary teachers.

3. Evaluation criteria: establish with the pupils how they would know if CDM was successful or not. These criteria could form the spokes of the wheel, attaching to the relating objectives.

So, for example, if pupils said that they thought they would enjoy lessons more if CDM was used, ask, 'How would we know?' Keep repeating this question until you all agree that you have found criteria that could be measured or evaluated in some way. The more pupils can be involved in the setting of criteria and the monitoring and evaluation, the better for all. They become researchers of their own experience, and teachers don't have to collect all the data themselves. For example, pupils might say that being more involved would be good because it would be fun (how would we know?), 'We would be smiling' (what else?), 'We would enjoy school more' (how would we know?), 'We wouldn't want to miss school' (how would we know?), 'The register would tell you' (what else?), 'we would probably want to do more work' (how would we know?).

Those of you working in countries where there is an established external monitoring system may be worried about how you might convince Ofsted inspectors – or your country's equivalent – of the impact of your CDM. This is important for schools and I hope that this book helps you to communicate your intentions, implementation and impact to Ofsted. Additionally, I want to focus on the involvement of staff and pupils in the *internal* monitoring of quality.

In-school public relations (PR)

In the early 1990s, I was seconded to the role of Parent Partnership Coordinator for a large Local Authority. I was responsible for working with schools and parents to improve the way we met and communicated about the special educational needs of children and young people. One of my jobs was to liaise with local voluntary organisations, parent groups and the local press to improve communication and policy-making. As part of my preparation for this role, I attended training on public relations (PR). It was well worth the time, and one particular lesson stayed with me: 'PR begins at home'. Your pupils and staff (all of them) have more influence on the way a school is viewed than any hand-picked PR team. Therefore it makes sense that time and resources are invested into making sure that the people *in* the school not only feel great about being there, and about the achievements of their school community, but that they are able and motivated to recognise and articulate it. What pupils and staff say about their school can be both positively powerful and extremely damaging, so it is as well to be aware of the messages they are giving others. It is useless to spend time on external PR if staff and pupils, who live and socialise locally, do not feel a sense of belonging and ownership.

So, before any talk of data collection for *external* scrutiny, it's important to know what staff and pupils are noticing about your school. What are staff and pupils noticing about each other? In a collaborative culture, people support each other to do the best job they can, because a great school is made up of lots of people doing just this.

Noticing together

People notice different things. I was visiting a school with Simon, an Educational Psychologist in training I was supporting, and we both agreed to *notice what we noticed* about a classroom we were visiting. Back in our office, we compared notes and found that we had noticed very different things. I had noticed that not only were the pupils talking with each other about the task in hand, but they were also complementing each other and making suggestions to each other about how the work could be done. Simon hadn't picked this up but had noticed immediately the make and model of the computer at the back of the classroom. I hadn't even noticed that there was a computer in the room, let alone clocked how recent a model it was. It didn't take me long to find out that Simon was very interested in computers and for Simon to discover that I was interested in pupil-to-pupil collaboration. Needless to say, after that visit I started to notice computers more and Simon started to listen out for pupil conversations. To make the most of the diverse ways in which different individuals within the school will notice things, we need to make sure that measures of progress and impact are open to observations of people with quite different perspectives to each other: staff and pupils.

What this means is that time needs to be scheduled at points in the year for collaborative quality-monitoring conversations to take place, where some consensus can be made within subject areas, year groups and the like about the quality of school life. This is an exercise which could well be run by a pupils-as-researchers group, once they have been trained up, or by a combined teacher-and-pupil research group. It does seem logical that those who experience the school's advantages and shortcomings – the pupils and teaching staff – should be key contributors to the planning and evaluation process. Professor Edie Holcomb, ex-head teacher and experience in school reform, commented that it was nonsense to teach critical thinking to pupils without expecting them to use these skills to assess their own schooling (Holcomb, 2012). If pupils are to develop such critical thinking skills, their teachers also need to model critical analysis of their own teaching. This is only possible in the safety of a collaborative school culture.

Three levels of monitoring and evaluation

CDM can be monitored using three groups of evidence, respectively, relating to:

- Sustained and extended use of CDM;
- Secondary outcomes mediated by CDM; and
- Improvements in the quality of processes and experiences, as a result of CDM.

Sustained and extended use of CDM

Research around pupil engagement tends to take one of two forms: studies that treat pupil engagement as an *independent* variable – studies that give pupils a voice and then find out what happens as a consequence – and those that treat pupil engagement as a *dependent* variable – looking into what needs to happen in order to increase pupil engagement in decision-making. This section focuses on CDM as an intended outcome that is itself dependent on other factors.

> Collaborative Decision-Making (CDM) is what happens when teachers and pupils make decisions together that affect the whole class or school. These decisions may be about community, curriculum, learning, recreation, discipline, the environment or resource and time management.
> A reminder of the definition used in the Introduction to this book

Useful baseline data can be collected and used to plot progress in the types and prevalence of CDM throughout the school. This might include:

- Data on pupils' responses to opportunities to be involved in decision-making such as a baseline measure of who is speaking in the classroom and how often;
- Teachers observing in each others' classrooms to identify CDM already in use and potential opportunities for CDM (see also Boyle, Fahey, Loughran, & Mitchell, 2001); and
- Organisational changes that have been made in the ways that school decisions are made.

Year groups or departments might keep a log of developments in place to document and exchange examples of CDM. Capture it using video, photos and documentation from discussions, and watch it grow:

Before, we used to...	Now we...	Soon we could...
Head of Dept selected books with teachers	Select three pupils by lottery to look at our selection before ordering.	Encourage older pupils to write materials for younger pupils.

Pupils can also take part in the evaluation of the impact of participation by keeping class logs and journals to document examples of collaboration – when and how these take place and the impact – and use this data for discussions between pupils and teachers as a valuable resource for learning. They might also contribute to the class what departmental logs described earlier. One school involved pupils in a discussion about how to measure pupil voice in their school, following which they developed their own 'voice-ometer'. Pupil representatives used this survey tool to ask pupils range of questions to find out how much of a say they felt they and other pupils had in the class and school in general. Another school used focus groups to find out what pupils thought about the various pupil voice initiatives that the school had developed, to help them to contribute to decision-making (Mayes, Finneran, & Black, 2018). Whilst it is challenging to find ways of representing impact to outsiders, it is important that within schools people feel that collaboration is happening, and is making difference.

Secondary outcomes mediated by CDM

Pupil engagement as leading to other things

It is quite possible that data relating to the secondary outcomes mentioned in the rationale section are already monitored on a regular basis. Schools are used to monitoring such things as attendance, academic outcomes and so forth. However, evaluation of school-level outcomes require a whole new approach if you are serious about collaboration, because meaningful collaboration engages staff and pupils as *joint* evaluators, and evaluation is seen as something done *by* them and *for* them, rather than as yet another thing that is done *to* them.

A group of pupils designed and collected 1,000 report card surveys evaluating teaching, counselling, school safety and facilities at three secondary schools. They wrote a report about the findings and recommendations. In the introduction to their report, they expressed their dissatisfaction with the current system for monitoring school quality: 'There are 48,000 youth in Oakland's schools that are experts – who are in class every day and who have a lot to say about how the schools are run and how to improve our education ... everyone wants to hear from the teachers and parents – but what about the students? Who asks our opinion? Why do we feel shut out, like no one cares what we think?' (Fletcher, 2005).

If pupils need to be involved in evaluating the processes that affect them, then teachers do too. If teacher workload or stress are amongst the CDM outcomes to the measured, then teachers need to be involved in defining and selecting metrics for these outcomes. This could be done in a focus group.

Questions might include:

■ How do you define 'workload'?

■ Is your workload okay right now, or do you have too much/too little to do outside lessons? How do you know?

■ How would you know if it had improved? How would others know?

■ What questions would help you to provide this information?

■ What ideas do you have for collecting this information?

Improvements in the quality of processes and experiences

The third type of impact concerns improvements in quality of processes and procedures that come about with CDM.

Total quality management

W. Edwards Deming is not a name you come across very often in staffroom conversations, but his legacy has a recognised relevance for schools (Crawford,

Bodine, & Hoglund, 1993; Williams, 2000). Deming was the father of Total Quality Management (TQM), the business model that turned around Japanese manufacturing in the 1980s. He observed that by the time a faulty product gets to the quality control department, it's too late to do anything but reject it – an expensive and wasteful option. Instead of accepting or rejecting goods at the end of the production line, with all the associated cost and wastage, Deming proposed that every part of the business and production line should be constantly monitored for quality. Deming's ideas have relevance for today's schools. By the time exam results and data on detentions, exclusions and attendance are out, there is little more you can do for the pupils involved. However, it is possible to regularly monitor the *quality* of the process: the start of the school day, lessons, staff meetings, assemblies, the lunchtime experience and so forth. The involvement of staff and pupils in assessing and improving the quality of all these school experiences is central to a school success.

Evaluations of the impact of CDM on the quality of processes might look something like this:

- A tutor–pupil group defined what a quality Registration would look like. As a result, shorter, news-based registration sessions were introduced, involving 'good gossip' and class-notes rota for absent classmates.

- All pupils who have been receiving additional support are now involved in CDM planning. This has led to new policies, including the eradication of segregated seating for pupils requiring additional assistance and adaptations to classroom processes which pupils said left them feeling marginalised, such as 'talking partners' and 'Golden Time'.

- CDM changed the way that attendance and punctuality records were organised to make it less de-motivating for pupils who had a bad start of term. Previously, pupils with poor initial attendance were defined by this data, even if they ended up with 100% attendance for the final term. Following CDM, a new policy meant that pupils could make a fresh start each month, and all pupils started each month with 100% attendance record, to encourage them to keep this up.

- A staff–pupil working group had looked at the role of school assemblies pupils carried out a short survey. A pilot set of pupil-led assemblies was planned, with pupil-evaluators planning a simple exit poll to get teacher and pupil feedback.

References

Boyle, S., Fahey, E., Loughran, J., & Mitchell, I. (2001). Classroom research into good learning behaviours. *Educational Action Research*, 9(2), 199–224. Retrieved from https://doi.org/10.1080/09650790100200149.

Crawford, D. K., Bodine, R. J., & Hoglund, R. G. (1993). *The school for quality learning: Managing the school and classroom the Deming way.* New York: Research Press.

Fletcher, A. (2005). *Meaningful student involvement: Guide to students as partners in school change.* Olympia WA: SoundOut Books. Retrieved from https://soundout.org/wp-content/uploads/2015/06/MSIGuide.pdf

Holcomb, E. L. (2012). *Data based decision-making.* Bloomington IN: Solution Tree Press.

Marr, B. (2020). Tesco: creating a corporate steering wheel. Retrieved March 26, 2020, from https://www.bernardmarr.com/default.asp?contentID=1052

Mayes, E., Finneran, R., & Black, R. (2018). *Victorian Student Representative Council (VicSRC) primary school engagement (PSE) evaluation final evaluation report PSE*. Melbourne, Australia.

Rowe, G. (2018) Democracy in the primary classroom. Unpublished thesis. UCL Institute of Education. Retrieved from: www.pupilparticipation.co.uk/resources

Williams, H. & Daniels, A. (2000). Framework for intervention part II: The road to total quality behaviour? *Educational Psychology in Practice: Theory, Research and Practice in Educational Psychology, 15*(4), 228–236.

4

Which decisions? Which pupils?

This chapter is divided into two sections. The first section covers the kinds of decisions that can be made by teachers in collaboration with their pupils. The second section looks at ways in which CDM can be considered appropriate for all pupils, irrespective of age, social background, ability or conduct.

Which decisions?

Article 12 of The United Nations Convention on the Rights of the Child states that children should be involved in all decisions that affect them (Committee on the Rights of the Child, 2009). It is hard to think of any school decision that does not affect pupils, so there is really no upper limit on such participation. However, for schools where CDM is still in its infancy, it is useful to have examples of the kind of decisions that teachers have been making using CDM. These include decisions relating to:

- Curriculum;
- Discipline;
- Environment;
- Time management;
- Resource selection and management;
- Policy and practice.

None of the three teachers who participated in my research was using CDM all of the time, which may be unsettling to those advocating a purist approach, but perhaps reassuring to those of you embarking on this as novices. It appears that pupils can be quite accepting of a mixed economy of collaborative and autocratic decision-making, but willingly rise to the occasion when invited to be involved in decision-making. Teachers tell me that once pupils feel safe to offer suggestions and to question established ways of doing things, it is quite a relief not to be the only person making all the decisions.

The use of CDM for decisions around *Negotiating the Curriculum* is covered in Chapter 6. This chapter continues with some examples of CDM being used for decisions about discipline, the classroom environment, time, resources and policies.

CDM and discipline

Research outlined in Chapter 2 described how the potential outcomes of CDM include improved teacher–pupil relationships and co-operation. In this chapter I describe some ways in which CDM can be used to improve discipline.

I once asked a group of six-year-olds what grown-ups did for them that they could do for themselves. Their list contained many unexpected contributions, and one of these went something like this: 'When we've had a quarrel and someone goes to tell the teacher, they always just say, "say sorry", and we might not be ready to say sorry, so that doesn't really help.' Carl learned a lot about himself and his pupils when he tried to let them sort out the classroom noise levels for themselves.

Positive outcomes

■ Carl's approach helped pupils to have an awareness of classroom sound levels and how these impact on learning, communication, concentration and well-being;

■ Pupils learned that they have communal responsibility for the noise levels in the classroom;

■ Pupils learnt that they are entitled to request and contribute to noise regulation in the classroom; and

■ The pupils started to self-regulate noise levels in the classroom.

STORY: SHUSHING

Participant Carl found it really annoying when pupils told each other to 'shush!' and he used to tell them, 'Don't, that just makes more noise. If you just look after yourself, slowly everyone will sense the mood and look after themselves and the classroom will be quiet.'

However, this didn't seem to be working and he decided that maybe if he could organise things so that the people who were 'loudest for longest' realised that they were really annoying everyone else, social pressure might mean that they would stop being so loud.

So he let them 'just argue a little bit about how to behave'. He believed that by discussing behaviour together, the children would be 'deepening their understanding of behaviour and how it is important to be quiet'. So he let them shush each other a lot more and let them have a go at each other and he 'just waited'. In the final interview he reported that it was not perfect, but that it was taking them less time to quieten than it had previously.

Carl realised that all these pupils had been conditioned to expect teachers to single-handedly monitor and control noise levels in the classroom.

Lessons learnt

- Sometimes the teacher has to relinquish the role of 'controller';
- For pupils to engage in change, they may have to be allowed to experience a period where they themselves are bothered by the problem;
- By inviting pupils to discuss behaviour as a class, teachers help pupils to act more responsibly. This has been reported by other researchers (e.g., Romi, Lewis, & Katz, 2009).

Ideas to consider

- Try a similar approach, but first tell your pupils that you want to stop nagging them about the noise and check they are okay with this;
- Give them a chance to self-regulate and have regular, brief updates on how things are going; and
- Discuss with your pupils what other ways you could collaborate with them over noise levels.

By letting children manage classroom disruption for themselves – sorting out friendship quarrels and break-time rows, pupils can learn important skills for solving

STORY: LESSON FROM SLOVENIA

Several years ago, I visited some schools in Slovenia as part of a European Union project on school leadership, and as part of this trip I spent a week in Ava's school, a state primary school catering for pupils aged seven to 14. Ava was timetabled to teach French and English to this particular class on alternate weeks. The lesson on the day I visited Ava's class visit was to have been French. Ava explained to the class that because I was visiting, she had decided to swap the lessons around to make this one English. The lesson began with an introduction to some new concepts from the teacher after which some tasks were set. Gradually, the pupils became more and more unruly, and I was concerned that my presence was the cause of this disruption.

Ava got the class's attention and said, 'This lesson doesn't seem to be going very well. Can we talk about it?' In the discussion that ensued, it became clear that they were confused and disgruntled because they had expected to come to a French lesson only to be told it had been changed. They said that it didn't feel right to just have that change made, and some of them had come with questions about the previous French lesson, or were looking forward to carrying on some work from last week, and now had to do something completely different. After five or 10 minutes' discussion, Ava asked the class what she and they could learn from today's experience. They said that they would like her to discuss any change of plan with them in future, rather than making such a decision on her own. Ava in turn said that she would really appreciate it if pupils would talk to her about dissatisfaction with a lesson, rather than keeping quiet about it but misbehaving. They agreed with each other's proposals and Ava invited them to write these agreements down in the back of their books, and she wrote it in the back of her book.

Typically, teachers respond to disruption by taking charge and telling pupils to stop messing around and get back to work. So this teacher's response was less usual, in experience. Interestingly, Ava told me she was highly embarrassed that I had witnessed a lesson where pupils were disruptive. On the contrary, I replied, this was one of the best secondary school lessons I had witnessed. I caught up with a couple of the pupils during lunchtime and asked them what they thought about what had happened in the lesson. They said it was actually one of the most satisfying lessons they'd had that week, as they really enjoyed discussing their experiences with the teacher; being treated as adults together.

interpersonal conflict and developing peaceful communities. However, pupils often need help to learn these skills, so practice with input from a teacher can be invaluable. Additionally, both pupils and teachers can learn from these conversations, as Slovenian teacher, Ava, discovered in the story above.

Ava learnt that

- It's okay to be vulnerable and admit you have made a mistake;
- Pupils are usually willing to take part in discussion;
- Pupils usually have some good points of view to express;
- Even well-prepared lessons need pupils on board;
- A teacher, like pupils, is always learning;
- I need to communicate more with my pupils about how and why I plan lessons;
- My pupils can't work when they feel confused or disrespected; and
- I enjoy these discussions.

Her pupils, in turn, learnt that

- Our teacher respects us and is prepared to listen to our views;
- She is human like us;
- For a lesson to go well, both teachers and pupils need to play their part;
- If we feel confused, it's best to talk about it rather than start misbehaving;
- There is usually a reason why we start messing around, and our teacher can help us to understand this better; and
- We enjoy these discussions.

Positive outcomes

- Not only had Ava taught them that when things are not going well, the best approach is to discuss it, but the pupils had also learnt how to express their views about a lesson and negotiate future ways of avoiding conflict; and
- Far from appearing a weak teacher, Ava had shown great confidence in addressing the problem in the way she had.

Lessons learnt

This small but memorable example illustrates the potential learning that takes place when collaborative discussion, avoiding any threats and coercion, is used to address classroom discipline problems. This example also shows how a teacher's courage and willingness to open up discussion about their own teaching can lead to mutual learning and improve the maturity of the relationship between a teacher and her class.

Ideas to consider

- If a disciplinary issue arises in the classroom, treat this as a learning opportunity and put by three to five minutes to talk with the class or group to find out what is happening;
- Model to the class that talking can help to clarify and resolve interpersonal conflict;
- Give this example to a class to read and ask them what they think of it, and whether such an approach might work in their class.

STORY: THE AWFUL MUSIC LESSON

Just before the end of term, research participant Michael had a music lesson with his class that was, in his opinion, 'just awful because they would not stop talking'. Michael sat down with them to talk about this: 'I need to talk to you about something ... I just personally don't feel that the way we are behaving as a class at the moment is very positive. I don't feel like it's very effective for our learning and I don't particularly enjoy being here. I'm not sitting here, standing here now to tell you off about it. I'm standing here to tell you how I feel. And what I would like you to do is talk about how you feel, and then we'll talk about that together.' They talked. They acknowledged that they were causing their teacher a lot of stress and were able to identify the additional work he had to do as a result. Having established that he was not the only one who was disturbed by the behaviour and felt it needed change, Michael addressed them, 'Okay, so that's our starting point then. You are all in agreement with me that the way we are behaving isn't okay. Put your hand up if, like – honestly, I'm not going to tell you off – put your hand up if you don't agree with that and if you think that the way the class, we are behaving is okay.'

When nobody responded, he invited them to think about ways of 'fixing the situation'.

Michael was surprised at how honest the children were, and particularly how they owned up to their own lapses in behaviour. At first all their suggestions were about things Michael could do, until he said that he had enough to do, and wanted to know what *they* could do to improve things. He asked them if they had done anything to help in their previous schools. They started talking about the jobs they used to do and what fun it was, and how they might start to do some of the same things in this school. As Michael didn't feel optimistic that this discussion would actually bring about any change, he followed this up with what he described as 'an authoritarian chat'. Michael spent a lot of time over the holiday thinking about what he could do with his class' behaviour. However, when they returned, he found that 'they just weren't like that anymore. It was really bizarre!'

Positive outcomes

- Behaviour improved;
- Michael felt positive about the conversation; and
- Pupils reflected with openness and accepting responsibility for their behaviour.

Lessons learnt

- Discussions like this can be enjoyable.
- Michael didn't lose any respect from pupils by being honest with them;
- Michael felt unsure of what he was doing – he might have benefitted from some support from a colleague with more experience of CDM at this stage;
- Pupils and teachers are often bothered by the same things; and
- It is worth giving discussions time to make a difference.

Ideas to consider

- When you are about to admonish or hand out a punishment to a class, ask them whether it would be more effective to discuss what is happening and what you could all do together to make things better.
- Have a 'practice run' to see how this kind of discussion works with a minor incident, rather than using it on a more serious one, in the same way that a chef would test out a new recipe on a friend or colleague, before serving it to a VIP!

Environment

One of my research participants reflected on the irony of teachers telling pupils at the start of the term, 'This is *your* classroom,' and then proceeding to make all the decisions about the room's layout, decoration, display, lighting and use themselves. There are more obvious opportunities for CDM around the classroom in primary than in secondary schools, where pupils move around from room to room. However, in secondary schools with a strong collaborative ethos, pupils may feel a sense of ownership over the whole school premises if they are empowered to do so. One Head of Art I worked with put a whole notice board by for pupils to display art they had done at home. The wide range of sketches, cartoon characters, paintings and photographs reflected a much wider range of artwork than she had seen through the formal lessons. A quiet girl, Louise, who had very poor attendance and rarely spoke to teachers, brought in some amazing manga art she had done at home. Louise started to get recognition from other pupils for her art and started to see school as a place she felt good about herself. A few months later, her large-scale manga representation of the Easter story was installed in the lobby of a local church.

I discovered the following story through a conversation with a secondary school teacher, Mrs Taylor, at a conference on Pupil Voice a few years ago.

STORY: MUDDY FLOORS

Mrs Taylor's Year 7 PSHE (Personal, Social and Health Education) class of 11- and 12-year-olds invited Mr Jordan, the caretaker (custodian), to come and talk to them about things they could do to improve the school building and grounds. He talked to them about the time it was taking him and the cleaners to clean the changing rooms, particularly when it had been raining. The class asked him questions such as: 'How much time does it take to clear the mud up? Would it save money for the school if we could help? Has this always been a problem?'

The pupils agreed that this was a problem for them also: 'When we are getting changed we don't want to stand on a muddy floor, and sometimes people slip over when it's muddy.' Mr Jordan wanted to know if they were interested in helping with the problem, and why. There was quite a lot of interest, particularly from the girls who said that it put them off using the changing room on rainy days, because the mud was 'smelly'. One pupil asked whether the problem was stopping the floors getting muddy in the first place, or finding better ways of cleaning it up. Mr Jordan opened this up to the class, who decided that it was better to look at ways of stopping the mud getting there in the first place.

Pupils started talking about how their local swimming pools and sports clubs had tackled this problem, such as wearing overshoes and having special matting along the walkways. Suddenly, one of the girls got excited and said that they had to do a design project, so why didn't they look at changing room design! Others joined in and said that maybe they could do some research on the Internet. Mr Jordan reminded them that there was currently no money available for this project, but if they found a way of saving on cleaning time, this might release some money. He asked the class what level of improvement they would be happy with. The general consensus was that they wanted to stand on a clean surface when they were getting changed.

Positive outcomes

- Pupils started to appreciate the work of Mr Jordan and the team of cleaners;
- Their respect for him grew and vice versa;
- They became more aware of the contribution they made to the muddiness of the floors; and
- They felt there was something they could do to improve their environment.

Lessons learnt

- Non-teaching staff can play their part in educational programmes;
- Both the class and Mr Jordan enjoyed the experience; and
- Pupils can come up with ideas within existing resources.

Ideas to consider

- Ask non-teaching staff for ideas for authentic problem-solving opportunities related to their work in school;
- Put areas of the school up for classes to 'bid for' making improvements to.

Many years ago I visited a classroom which was stunningly child-designed – all the labels and signs had been designed and made by the six-year-olds themselves. Various objects and highly original art creations were displayed on wall-mounted boxes and homemade shelves, each 'labelled' by pupils in their own way. I had not seen such imaginative display ideas in a classroom before. I learnt that the teacher had invited a curator from the local museum to help her to teach the children some skills of display and design. From that time, they had curated their own exhibitions and displays, and had even started to think about lighting and audio to enhance their displays, as this was something the curator had demonstrated on a museum visit.

STORY: MRS FINTELMAN'S CLASSROOM

Some teachers really enjoy getting the classroom ready for the new class of pupils, and feel this gets the term off to a good start. However, teacher Emily Fintelman doesn't do this. She believes that children learn best when they have real ownership of their classroom. She considers that 'theming' your classroom before term marks the room as the teacher's territory, rather than the pupils'.

Here are Emily's tips to enable pupils to set up their own space at the start of the year:

- Leave the room as bare are you can before pupils arrive;
- Organise resources such as books and furniture but don't place them;
- Engage the class in detailed discussions on what a learning space actually *needs* – Emily contributes her own perspective where pupils have not thought about potential activities;
- Get pupils to reflect on what they might do in their room, and what they might need for these activities. Once again, Emily adds her own suggestions;
- Emily is careful to ask, 'What do you think helps you learn best in a classroom?' rather than 'What do you want in your classroom?' to avoid the popular yet unrealistic dream of a classroom rollercoaster or bouncy castle!
- In small groups, consider all the ideas and draw pictures of how the space could be used to best suit the tasks identified; and
- Make sure pupils know that any decision is collective, and not final, as changes will often be made as they identify a need. Help them to accept that it won't be perfect (adapted from Fintelman, 2019).

Emily reported how one class described the room, before they had made a start on their collaborative plan, as 'dull, boring and plain'. However, after setting it up themselves, they thought it was 'exciting, helpful and fun'. These pupils concluded that all teachers should let pupils set up their own room the way they like it, so that they feel it really is their own space, rather than a room that belongs to their teacher.

Reflecting on the space and its use for learning, Emily recognised that she and fellow teachers sometimes take up too much space in the classroom. So each year, she challenges herself to take up half as much room as she did the previous year. Her aim is to reduce the space she takes up each year, until she doesn't even have an 'area' of her own.

Positive outcomes

- Pupils learn about design, management and use of space and resources;
- They are more likely to feel responsible for a space they have planned; and
- Pupils take pride in something they have designed.

Lessons learnt

- When resources are managed by pupils, teachers don't need to organise and manage them; and
- Pupils are able to design classroom layouts to reflect their own learning.

Ideas to consider

- Involve pupils in setting up their own classroom as Emily did;
- Give pupils their own display board(s);
- Teach them display skills – visit museums, shops, galleries to see different approaches to display design and curation;
- Invite pupils to take and display photos of themselves enjoying school and classroom activities;
- Ask pupils to design and create resources for displays;
- Encouraging pupils to bring in artwork and personal projects they have completed at home to display in class.

Time management

The control over use of one's own time has been identified as a powerful motivator in the workplace. However, I have yet to find an example of CDM involving time management, apart from the ubiquitous, 'Does anybody want more time on this?' type question. Therefore, I will have to imagine what it might look like. Teachers are managing time continually, so there is no reason why these decisions shouldn't be collaborative. How else are pupils going to learn to take responsibility for the use of time? Many time-related decisions in the classroom are taken dynamically, as teachers continually assess what is possible in the time available: for example, have we got time for one more thing or should we go over what we have done today? If teachers make all these decisions themselves, pupils miss out on valuable opportunities to develop their own time-management skills.

The starting point is for teaching staff to be aware of the time-related decisions they are making already. Maybe you could talk to your pupils about the whole issue of time management, discuss the time-related decisions you are currently making before, during and after a lesson, and ask them for ways that they could be more involved in this decision-making.

Ideas to consider

Start to build awareness of how long things take and put control of time back in pupils' hands: e.g.

- We have two tasks to complete today. Do you think that these two tasks will take the same amount of time?
- So how much time should we give this task?
- What if some people don't finish in that time?
- Should we try to get through this today or stretch it out over a week?
- Should we do it at home?

Resource management

The selection, storage, care and management of resources provide great learning opportunities for pupils, and are available in every classroom and school. The following story concerns CDM with a group of pre-school children on how to spend a budget for toys. I hope that teachers of much older pupils might be inspired to find ways to make related decisions with their own pupils.

STORY: SHOPPING FOR TOYS

Early-years workers invited a group of two- to four-year-olds to help them to choose new toys for their crèche. They sat down and looked at toyshop catalogues with these four children and talked about the toys in the pictures. Children picked out those that they had at home and talked about toys it would be nice to have in the crèche.

As they had a budget of £30, they put 30 discs in a box. As they selected toys, they counted out the number of discs equal to the amount. Through counting out the 'money', the children could see that certain toys were beyond their budget, and that choices would need to be made between other toys. Through this discussion the children were able to use their imagination and reflect on their own experiences with toys, both in the crèche and at home. One boy said that if there were more footballs there wouldn't be so many fights; others talked about the toys they had noticed other children enjoying; and all of them described how they might play with toys in the catalogue. They discussed the details of the shopping trip they would make to buy these toys and, together with two of the workers, caught the bus into town and bought the toys.

Positive outcomes

- The children started to appreciate the relative cost of the toys, and to select ones that fitted their budget;
- They used counting in an authentic, real-life, task;
- They practised negotiation, communication and decision-making skills; and
- They learned that they could have a say in decisions about their toys.

Lessons learnt

- Even very young children can consider the needs of the whole group, not just their own;
- Two- to four-year-olds are able to imagine how resources might be used by the group, and how they might create or solve conflict;
- All children are able to take part in their own way, whilst learning from each other; and
- Reflection and forward planning can be practised using authentic tasks.

Ideas to consider

- Carry out a similar exercise with older pupils, using stationery, furniture or technology catalogues or websites;
- For school leaders – share budgetary information with staff or senior pupils and use a similar collaborative approach for budgetary decisions;
- Run a session for parents and carers to encourage them to involve children in family decision-making in a similar way.

Simply asking young children what they think is unlikely to work

- Some children will not understand the question or why you are asking it – they need to understand the aim of the exercise;
- Some may be more interested in pleasing you than expressing what they feel, and will try to guess what answer you want to hear;
- Some children will not be able to express themselves verbally – so you need to use visual methods, movement and gesture, as well as stories, drama and dialogue;
- Just because children enjoy taking part in a consultation doesn't necessarily mean that you are eliciting their preferences – they may just enjoy the activity;
- For children to express real preferences, they need to have experienced the choices on offer; and
- Children need to understand the factors that are involved in making decisions – asking what they would like and then offering something different can leave them feeling like they and their views don't really count.

(Adapted from Miller, 1997)

Policy and practice

It might be a while before you are ready for using CDM for school policy and process decisions, but it might not be as daunting as some people think. One example of such decision-making took place in a small middle school. Teachers started off by using pupils as researchers to gather data about pupil views, but they didn't stop there. The pupil researchers were invited to join staff in curriculum planning meetings, where they collaborated with teachers to design programmes of work. Working as partners with staff gave the pupils the confidence to want to collaborate

STORY: PUPIL-LED PARENTS' EVENINGS (PARENT–TEACHER CONFERENCES)

The teaching staff were reviewing their parents' evenings (parent–teacher conferences) and felt less than happy with them, especially as many of their 11- to 14-year-old pupils didn't even turn up. They decided to ask pupils for their ideas about how these meetings could be improved. The first thing that pupils told them was that parents never heard anything new at these meetings: 'Dan could do better if he paid more attention,' 'Ali doesn't do her homework,' 'Tim talks too much in class,' and so forth. Pupils felt that comments like these often led to parents nagging or punishing them, and suggested that instead of focusing on what needed to *change*, that the meetings should focus on what was going *well*. The teachers agreed that the forthcoming meetings with parents would focus on what pupils identified as their best five or six pieces of work, using their own criteria. Other work could be made available to parents after the meeting if needed.

The plan they followed:

- Each pupil will be handed their own meeting folder by the teacher, containing: (1) the written self-evaluation, (2) the official school report card and (3) the 'best work'.
- Pupils can begin the conference with a discussion of any of the three sections of the folder.
- At some point in the discussion, however, they must describe what they have been studying and show the related work, highlighting their best work.
- Parents will most probably ask clarifying questions to prompt pupils to offer additional information.
- The written self-evaluation can be read aloud by the pupil or given to the parent to read.
- Goals must be discussed.
- Teachers will enter the conversation only as needed.

(Adapted from Apple & Beane, 2007)

Although some teachers felt under-prepared and had some doubts about this plan – not confident that these pupils could lead their own meetings and unsure whether parents really wanted to come to a parents' evening to listen to their own child – the plan went ahead.

The first pupil, an able girl who did good work but didn't join in group discussions, sat down and introduced her mother and sister then started to talk about her best work, and read her self-evaluation to her mother. Without prompting from the teacher, her mother asked her why she didn't want to join in discussions and why homework needed to be done away from the TV. All her teacher had to do was validate what the pupil and her mother were saying.

With this pupil and others, the pupils controlled the direction of the discussion from the introductions to wrapping them up at the agreed time. The participating teachers found that pupils were well able to describe their own strengths and weaknesses; in many cases, staff had to step in to soften their over-harsh self-assessments. Most of them could point out what they were good at and what needed more work.

on wider school issues, so they requested a meeting with the school principal to advocate for changes in the way the school approached discipline and physical education. (SooHoo, 1993, quoted in Fletcher, 2005)

The story above involves a school making changes to their parent consultation evenings, which had been very teacher-led in the past. Although pupils were not involved in decisions about this change, the new format for these consultations involved a much more collaborative event than had previously been the case.

This example took place in a school where pupil voice was already a priority in the school development plan, so there was an acceptance that CDM was something that was going to be supported by the senior leadership.

For some of the pupils, this parents' evening may have been the first time they have had such an in-depth discussion with their parents about their schoolwork. By inviting pupils to lead their own meetings, the school has given some strong messages to pupils: This is about you; this is your life; these are your decisions.

Dissatisfaction was an important part of change – It is important to note that the starting point for this change was dissatisfaction with the current arrangements for parents' evenings. Psychologists who study the process of educational change have found that for change to become embedded in an organisational culture, there needs first to be a recognition that the existing practice is either redundant – such as boys and girls using separate school entrances – or no longer available – for example, corporal punishment is no longer an option in most countries (Blikstein, 2013; Marzano, Zaffron, Zraik, Robbins, & Yoon, 1995).

Positive outcomes

- Pupils spoke with enthusiasm and confidence about their work;
- Pupils and their parents engaged in more detailed and in-depth discussions about their learning than in any previous meetings;
- There was a lot of humour, and all involved enjoyed the experience and wanted to repeat it; and
- Pupils felt special.

Lessons learnt

- This meeting format seemed to work well – it put pupils in charge of what and how things were said, and all the information that would have been exchanged in the old meetings was more than covered; and
- Some teachers and pupils who initially struggled with the change of role, still agreed that it had worked.

Ideas to consider

- Discuss this parents' evening format with a group of pupils, parents and staff to see how your school might do something similar; and
- List processes in your class or school that could do with a bit of modernisation, and involve pupils in considering a new collaborative approach.

Which pupils?

I believe that CDM is relevant for all children, and that imagination is needed to rethink schooling for some groups of pupils. The populations I address in this section have been chosen to reflect the groups of pupils who often miss out on opportunities to have a say in how schools are run. These are often the very children and adolescents whose voice we need to include in our decision-making. The section headings reflect the kinds of questions I have been asked by school staff when I have raised the subject of collaboration:

- For rich and poor children?
- For all ages?
- For all abilities?
- Only for the well-behaved?

Where I can, I have incorporated some teachers' stories as examples of CDM use with groups who sometimes get fewer opportunities for CDM at school.

For rich and poor children?

Even though you thoroughly approve of involving children in decision-making, you may feel that this is only possible in small classes with high-achieving, well-behaved children with highly supportive parents. Fortunately for those teachers wanting to try CDM with children from across the socio-economic population, there is a rich, international tradition of progressive education – including names such as Dewey, Holmes, Lane, Bloom, Freire, Rousseau, Freinet, Pestalozzi, Montessori and Froebel – where collaborative approaches have been used successfully with children from the most disadvantaged sectors of society to the most privileged. Elsewhere, CDM has been beneficial for children who suffer quite severe and long-term deprivation (Hart, 1992; Shier, 2009). Research into more participative approaches to teaching suggests that all children benefit from CDM, but those who benefit the most are those from disadvantaged homes (Alexander, 2016; Bell, 2017; Marmot & Bell, 2012).

For all ages?

Children as young as three years old are capable of thoughtful decision-making and can be involved in CDM, although some skill may be needed on the adult's part to adapt techniques to suit very young children, or children who are developmentally young for their age (Epstein, 2003).

My own work with young children, as an EP, has been influenced by the work of Alison Clarke, in particular, her Mosaic Approach – a framework to help adults to find out about and incorporate young children's views, perceptions and wishes into their planning (Clark, 2001). One of Clarke's techniques was to give young children a simple camera and invite them to take photos of anything around the nursery that they found interesting. She then used these pictures for discussion. Through similar exercises I have learnt a lot about how children view their environment. For example, I remember a session where a group of four-year-olds were looking at a photo one of

STORY: LEARNING ABOUT WHALES

Ron Nelson, Assistant Professor of Applied Psychology, and Lin Frederick, first grade teacher, carried out a year-long curriculum-making project with six- and seven-year-olds in a primary school where over 50 per cent of children received free school meals. Lin started by putting together a list of themes that would cover the prescribed curriculum objectives. She had made a judgement or theme she felt would interest her class, but checked this out with them through class discussions in which they talked about what they already knew and how these themes linked to the things they had learnt before.

Through 20 minutes discussion each day, they identified a theme for each two-week unit, explored questions related to that theme and decided on the following week's activities. Through these discussions, Lin was able to judge the interest level, background knowledge and connections to previous learning, and to find out what information pupils considered important or wanted to find out. They also use these sessions to form curriculum questions.

Lin used an interdisciplinary curriculum wheel to help the class learn that any single theme had lots of different aspects that could be explored. The wheel had the theme for the unit as its hub – for example, 'Whales' – and the six spokes represented the curriculum areas of: maths, art, social sciences, language arts, geography and science. The wheel wasn't used to get an even spread of questions across the disciplines, but rather to expand areas of investigation that children might not have considered by themselves.

The class discussed the different types of question and were able to categorise and colour code questions from their brainstorm and these headings. For example, pupils collaborated with Lin to devise following questions for their unit on whales:

1 [Recall] What are the basic facts about whales?
2 [Analysis] What are the characteristics of whales?
3 [Comparison] How are whales the same and different from each other and from other species?
4 [Inference] Why do whales live in the oceans?
5 [Evaluation] Should whales be captured for zoos?

(Nelson & Frederick, 1994)

The pupils then suggested activities that could be used to help them learn these things. I loved it that one boy suggested they just go outside and 'play at being whales'!

When Ron later tested the same procedure with 10- to 11-year-olds, he found that the whole-class tasks of identifying questions and agreeing instructional approaches – that had taken two sessions to cover with the younger children - could be collapsed into a single session.

them had taken of what looked like an ordinary path through the school grounds. I asked the child who had taken the photograph to talk about it. He said that this was one of his favourite parts of the school, because it was where the best twigs were to be found for making bug hotels. The other children joined in and talked about other parts of school grounds that they like or disliked. Who would ever have known that a picture of a path could unleash so much valuable discussion, and give adults a real child's-eye view of the school? Exercises like this have provided teachers with significant and otherwise obscure information that have helped them to make improvements to the school and classroom. I have found that many of the techniques developed by and for early-years' educators can be adapted for older pupils, those with learning difficulties or delay and even for pupils in higher education (George, 2009; Miller, 1997).

What drew my attention to the story above, Learning about Whales, was the combination of quite sophisticated metacognition concepts – question types and the curriculum wheel – with children's own expertise on how they learn.

Positive outcomes

- Pupils were able to identify which learning approaches worked for them;
- They became skilled in the language, processes and constraints of problem-solving;
- Across all ability levels, the curriculum was covered and objectives met for every child;
- They became quite sophisticated in analysing and understanding the role of different types of questions and knowledge; and
- Pupils started to recognise the relevance of different activities for learning different skills and knowledge.

Lessons learnt

- Even within a prescribed curriculum, there is flexibility for negotiation with pupils;
- Children as young as six years old can categorise questions and use a curriculum wheel;
- The curriculum design process can be adapted for different age groups; and
- Children like to learn through play and pictures, when given the chance.

Ideas to consider

- Make your own curriculum wheel;
- Colour-code different types of questions on class brainstorms;
- Partner up with a less-confident teacher to pilot new approaches;
- Hold an event for parents to describe the new approach.

For all abilities?

Two of the participants in my research study, Carl and Michael, came to my attention because of the way in which they were using CDM to support individuals and groups of pupils who by their conduct or learning difficulties were failing to thrive in the classroom (Rowe, 2018). Several teachers have told me that when they work collaboratively with their class, that the quiet or previously marginalised pupils surprise them with their new levels of participation. This seems to be a virtuous cycle of trust, risk-taking, support and confidence once pupils realise that they can influence what goes on in their classroom and beyond. In the same way that approaches need to be adapted for different age groups, so it is with different abilities. Prof. Richard Andrews proposes that education should help children to argue well, so that they can challenge conventional ideas and come up with their own new ones, and in so doing, transform not only their classrooms and schools but society (Andrews, 2009).

Professor Andrews has made a study of the development of argument skills in children. He identifies some developmental steps which could easily serve as a hierarchy of objectives for children's ability to collaborate in decision-making:

- Pre-verbal – a) physical struggles; b) voiced assertions.
- Asserts opinions a) e.g., I want … b) with single reason c) a number of reasons.
- Takes on board opposing argument.
- Sustains an argument at length.
- Considers both sides of an argument.
- Deliberates – makes a judgement after much thought.
- Is aware of dialectical processes – understands the question-and-answer *progression*.

(Adapted from Andrews, 1995)

An awareness of the development of these skills in children helps teachers to plot the progress of skills and confidence of both individuals and the whole class. This enables staff to develop ways of enhancing pupil skills and confidence, and provides a vocabulary for staff discussions around making decision-making a curriculum outcome.

A framework like this may well have helped the teachers in my next story. 'New listening' illustrates how staff in a special-needs school went about increasing their pupils' involvement in decision-making, including the challenges of giving a voice to children with no verbal language.

STORY: NEW LISTENING

The leadership team of a special-needs school for pupils aged 5–11 wanted to improve the way they included pupil voice and decision-making power right across the school (Harrison, 2019). With very few examples of how to do this in a school where many pupils had limited or no verbal skills, they knew that they had a big challenge on their hands. In particular, they needed to find a way to support open and honest interactions between pupils, staff, parents and the wider community, without leading the pupils or speaking for them.

One of the senior leaders started up a Student Voice Group in which they used picture cards, voice output devices and keyword signing to communicate. Their topics included: having a voice, sharing ideas, being friends, helping each other and teamwork. Group members were selected from across the ability range – including some non-verbal pupils – paying attention to which pupils would get along and a few more confident pupils who could provide a model for other pupils.

The member of staff learnt a lot from meetings with this group. At first, pupils just stared and looked confused when asked open questions such as, 'What do you all think about X or Y?' She realised that she needed to build up pupils' confidence so she did this by offering them lots of practice of 'thumbs up/down' voting. This helped the pupils to understand how voting worked, that their opinions were taken seriously and that *they* could make decisions. They began voting on as many things as they could: what games to play, what colour to use, what sticker, what song, what actions, etc. At first, pupils just looked at each other to see how their friends were voting, but gradually pupils started to realise that they had a personal power to influence how decisions were mad. This was celebrated at a meeting when, for the first time, one pupil voted 'no' when the rest of the group voted 'yes'.

The Group was invited to run certain aspects of the whole school weekly assembly. They started with small things, like signing as a song was being sung. This led to the Group taking bigger responsibilities such as setting up and running the PA system, creating Spotify playlists for use in assembly, and dismissing classes at the end of assembly.

The staff and those pupils involved had learnt a lot through the Student Voice Group, but the plan had always been to bring pupils into decision-making right across the school, in their own classrooms. The starting point for this was staff development, so senior leaders opened up staff discussions around the importance of collaborative decision-making for their particular population of pupils, and what this might look like for pupils with such a varied range of communication abilities.

Their staff discussions covered the following topics:

- What voice and agency looks like for our pupils.
- Voice and decision-making as body language.
- Choice-making, communication systems, eye contact.
- Independence.
- Artistic expression.
- How are we listening to pupils?
- How can we collaborate with pupils plan our teaching?

Through these discussions, staff started to really value what they were already doing, but also realised how much more they could be doing. Teachers started to take steps to find out much more about the pupils in their class and discovered that what they, the teachers, felt was working well, was not always viewed in the same way by pupils.

The school leadership team started out to challenge the notion that pupils like theirs are often invisible to the outside world. They realised that any pupil voice initiative would also require a change in perceptions and expectations of staff, parents and the pupils themselves. For example, we are told that one mother called in to ask why her daughter had been chosen for the Student Voice Group when she couldn't even talk!

What I liked about this story is the really big vision that the school leadership had for their pupils: to raise the visibility and influence of children and young people by really listening to and acting on the views of individuals and communities who may otherwise remain invisible and unheard. They were undaunted by early challenges, and senior leaders showed an awareness that the whole school culture needed to change, and the dedication to persist with those changes. There seems to have been a real sense of 'we are all finding out about this voice thing together' and staff being open to learning from their pupils. It also sounds like they were having a lot of fun along the way. That parent who didn't believe that her daughter was capable of being in a pupil voice group may be representative of many other parents, so it would be interesting to know if she has now changed her views about her daughter's capabilities, or started to include her more in decision-making at home.

Positive outcomes

- Perceptions and expectations of pupils, staff and parents were raised; and
- Pupils learnt new communication skills and increased in confidence.

Lessons learnt

- Trying out approaches with a small group of selected pupils helps to identify what will work with the larger population of pupils;
- If you start with simple things and get confident with these, other, bolder approaches will be less daunting;
- Parents' perceptions and expectations may need challenging, and maybe the school modelling trust and confidence in pupils is the first step;
- Practitioners need to devise ways for younger and developmentally young pupils to voice their opinions and views that do not depend on written and verbal models; and
- Practitioners need to develop the skills of how to listen and understand children's verbal and non-verbal communication, especially to younger pupils and those less likely to be heard at school.

Ideas to consider

- Base a staff or staff-pupil discussion on the story above;
- Use your school council or similar group, to discuss ways to involve all pupils in school decision-making, and to make CDM in classrooms part of every pupil's experience;
- Select pupils by lottery to have a voice, make a choice or do a job, so that every pupil gets a chance to experience status and empowerment.

Only for the well-behaved?

There may be times when battle lines are drawn between some pupils and teachers. Rather than making these pupils an exception to collaboration, these are the very pupils where collaboration can be at its most potent. Nelson Mandela once said that the best way to deal with one's enemies was to work alongside them and in that way turn animosity into partnership. Showing respect to so-called 'troublesome' pupils by listening to them and using their ideas can help them to see their teachers as power-givers rather than people who take their power away through punishment and coercion.

In my conversations with those pupils who are regularly in trouble for their misconduct, I find that they often express appreciation for those teachers who are open and sincere about what they do. These teachers show an interest in pupils' lives and are prepared, in turn, to share their own interests with pupils. In this way, pupils start to see their teachers as fellow human beings, and vice versa, not just as people occupying a role. I have seen relationships between teachers and pupils improve dramatically when they have recognised skills and interests in each other that they value. Albert Bandura's Social Learning Theory explains that a pupil is more likely to copy or be influenced by a teacher if they perceive that teacher to be similar to themselves in some way (Bandura, 1977). The pupils who get into trouble in school are, arguably, the ones that teachers need to have the best relationship with if they are to be influential. By collaborating with these pupils, teachers are showing respect and breaking down the pupil–teacher distinctions.

A pupil interviewed in a pupil voice project on teaching and learning highlighted how some working-class pupils feel stigmatised because of the way they talk. These pupils can easily feel that their opinions hold less weight than those of pupils who speak like the teachers (Fielding & Rudduck, 2002).

There are other ways in which children from poor families feel marginalised, and it is maybe not surprising that these children benefit the most from being involved in decision-making. By being listened to, pupils feel valued and are more likely to want to come to school and engage in lessons. I remember many years ago helping a school to carry out some research with a group of Year 10 pupils who were close to exclusion. Teachers were surprised to learn that some pupils with very poor attendance – who they doubted would turn up for the discussion session – came to school on those days when they knew that their opinions were going to be sought. Again, when I was running a students-as-researchers project in a secondary school with a similarly identified group of boys, I saw how much they relished the chance to offer their views about school life. I also discovered that we can learn a lot about our schools and classrooms when we listen to these pupils.

References

Alexander, R. (2016). What works and what matters: Education in spite of policy. In *CPRT Conference: What Is and What Might Be* (pp. 1–17). Cambridge Primary Review Trust. Retrieved from http://www.robinalexander.org.uk/wp-content/uploads/2016/11/Alexander-CPRT-keynote-final1.pdf

Andrews, R. (1995). *Teaching and learning argument*. London: Cassell.

Andrews, R. (2009). *The importance of argument in education. Inaugural lecture*. Institute of Education, University of London. Retrieved from http://citeseerx.ist.psu.edu/viewdoc/download?doi=10.1.1.465.7159&rep=rep1&type=pdf

Apple, M. W., & Beane, J. A. (Eds.). (2007). *Democratic schools: Lessons in powerful education* (2nd ed.). Portsmouth, NH: Heinemann. Retrieved from http://www.eklavya.in/pdfs/Books/demobratic Schools.pdf

Bandura, A. (1977). *Social learning theory*. Englewood Cliffs, NJ: Prentice Hall.

Bell, R. (2017). *Psychosocial pathways and health outcomes: Informing action on health inequalities*. London: Public Health England. Retrieved from www.gov.uk/phe%0Awww.gov.uk/phe

Blikstein, P. (2013). Seymour Papert's Legacy: Thinking About Learning, and Learning About Thinking. Retrieved December 29, 2015, from https://tltl.stanford.edu/content/seymour-papert-s-legacy-thinking-about-learning-and-learning-about-thinking

Clark, A. (2001). *Transforming children's spaces: Children's and adults' participation in designing learning environments*. London: Routledge. Retrieved from https://books.google.co.uk/books?hl=e n&lr=&id=WyWMAgAAQBAJ&oi=fnd&pg=PP1&dq=Clark,+A.+(2010)+Transforming+ Children's+Spaces:+Children's+and+adults'+participation+in+designing+learning+environ ments,+London,+Routledge.&ots=_Cg1vNRYK-&sig=KznlaQWN98BrUBBNEUC

Committee on the rights of the Child. (2009). *General Comment no. 12: The right of the child to be heard* (Vol. 12). Geneva. Retrieved from http://www2.ohchr.org/english/bodies/crc/ docs/AdvanceVersions/CRC-C-GC-12.pdf

Epstein, A. S. (2003). How planning and reflection develop young children's thinking skills. *Young Children*, (September), 58(5) 1–8. Retrieved from https://www.brandeis.edu/lemberg/ employees/pdf/planningandreflection.pdf

Fielding, M., & Rudduck, J. (2002). The Transformative Potential of Student Voice: Confronting the Power Issues. *Paper Presented at the Annual Conference of the British Research Association, University of Exeter, England, 12–14 September 2002. Consultation, Community and Democratic Tradition Symposium*. https://doi.org/10.1016/j.puhe.2007.04.008

Fintelman, E. (2019). How to Let Your Students Set up Their Own Classroom. Retrieved February 23, 2020, from http://mrsfintelmanteaches.global2.vic.edu.au/2017/03/06/ students-set-up-their-own-classroom/

Fletcher, A. (2005). *Meaningful student involvement: Guide to students as partners in school change*. Olympia: WA.

George, S. (2009). Too Young for respect? Realising Respect for Young Children in Their Everyday Environments – a Cross-Cultural Analysis. *Working Papers in Early Childhood Development, 54*. Retrieved from http://www.portaldahabitacao.pt/opencms/export/sites/ intranet/pt/intranet/documentos/gepa/2010/0119_doc_too_young_for_respect.pdf

Harrison, N. (2019). Student voice: Successes and challenges. *Connect, June*(237), 18–20. Retrieved from https://research.acer.edu.au/cgi/viewcontent.cgi?article=1246&context=connect

Hart, R. A. (1992). *Children's participation: From tokenism to citizenship. UNICEF: Innocenti Essays* (Vol. 4). Florence. https://doi.org/88-85401-05-8

Marmot, M., & Bell, R. (2012). Fair society, healthy lives: Strategic review of health inequalities in England post-2010. *Public Health, 126*(*Suppl*), S4–10.

Marzano, R. J., Zaffron, S., Zraik, L., Robbins, S. L., & Yoon, L. (1995). A new paradigm for educational change. *Education, 116*(2), 162–173. Retrieved from http://proquest.umi.com/ pqdlink?did=9377516&sid=1&Fmt=2&clientId=17822&RQT=309&VName=PQD%5Cn papers3://publication/uuid/8D51DD93-7641-45A3-942C-A51FC3EED6CA.

Miller, J. (1997). *Never too young: How young children can take responsibility and make decisions*. London: National Early Years Network & Save the Children.

Nelson, J., & Frederick, L. (1994). Can children design curriculum? *Teaching for Understanding, 51*(5), 71–74. Retrieved from http://www.ascd.org/publications/educational-leadership/ feb94/vol51/num05/Can-Children-Design-Curriculum¢.aspx.

Romi, S., Lewis, R., &Katz, Y. J. (2009). Student responsibility and classroom discipline in Australia, China, and Israel. *Compare: A Journal of Comparative and International Education, 39*(4), 439–453.

Rowe, G. (2018) Democracy in the primary classroom. Unpublished thesis. UCL Institute of Education. Retrieved from: www.pupilparticipation.co.uk/resources

Shier, H. (2009). 'Pathways to participation' revisited: Learning from Nicaragua's child coffee workers. In B. Percy-Smith (Ed.), *A handbook of children and young people's participation paperback*. London: Routledge.

SooHoo, S. (1993). Students as partners in research and restructuring schools. *The Educational Forum, 57*(15), 386–393.

5

How to collaborate

The teachers in my study (Rowe, 2018) had no guidance or training in CDM and were very much making it up as they went along. The type of CDM they were most commonly using was in the design and adaptation of routines and processes, such as when Carl stopped sorting his class into teams and groups and encouraged them to do this amongst themselves. Sometimes participants devised routines to enable pupils to start to be involved in decision-making. For example, Carl introduced some fun voting techniques, and Philip made use of his existing philosophy sessions to help pupils become more confident in expressing their opinions in whole class discussions. Sometimes routines were devised *with* pupils, and sometimes pupils suggested new ways of doing things. Once they got used to this two-way exchange of ideas, pupils spontaneously started to suggest new ways for the teacher or class to do things, such as in Carl's Fox Poo Check story in Chapter 1.

All participants found CDM a good way of problem-solving issues as they arose in the classroom. When there was a problem with behaviour, curriculum, equipment or time, these teachers would discuss it with their classes, first to see if the pupils were as concerned as they were about the issue, and then to come up with a solution together.

Before introducing any formal CDM, all participants in my research study made sure that the classroom ethos was one where pupils would feel free to talk openly about themselves and their experiences, wishes, ideas and opinions. I can't stress how important a safe and trusting classroom culture is for CDM to thrive, and Chapter 7 covers the topic in more detail.

Questions teachers frequently ask me include: How do you stop the vocal, confident children from dominating the discussion and decision-making? Does CDM mean you hand all your power to children? Where will we find the time?

Understandably, teachers worry about a small number of strong voices dominating classroom discussions, and the quieter, less confident children being left out. This is true for all class discussions, and sometimes teachers will find it useful to use a structure for class discussions, such as described in Class Meetings below, or, as participant Philip did in his philosophy-based sessions, teach the class a formal set of communication gestures to show when they wish to speak, agree or disagree with another speaker, or are just listening. Participants in my research study were surprised to find that pupils who had rarely taken part in other class discussions started to speak up once they were asked to talk about their own experiences. This is reflected in other research (e.g., Brough, 2012; Cox & Robinson-Pant, 2008). It does seem that children who are not quite sure about their facts when talking about conventional curriculum topics become more confident once they are talking about the subject they are experts in – their own experiences.

Participant Carl devised small, impromptu approaches to get his pupils more involved in the ongoing decision-making that is part of classroom life. However, as CDM became part of the classroom ethos, Carl described the decision-making interactions between him and his class as 'a conversation that they've always been having'. That is, everything is up for review and improvement, using pupils' observations and ideas.

Although CDM is an educational philosophy, rather than an 'approach' or 'method', it can be useful to have an idea about how other teachers have put this philosophy into practice. I offer these examples not for you to copy, but to inspire and stimulate you and your pupils to come up with something new for yourselves. The procedures that have been employed by teachers for CDM include the following, many of which are illustrated by stories throughout this book:

- Class meetings
- Problem-solving
- The informal plenary
- Voting
- Randomly-selected decision-makers
- Students-as-researchers
- Opportunistic CDM
- Digital technologies

Class meetings

Weekly meetings in the classroom enable pupils to say how they would like to organise things in their classroom. Such a meeting might take the following form:

- Start with a highlight of the week;
- Pupils are invited to put anything on the agenda; and
- The teacher chairs the meeting initially, then gradually steps back as pupils learn how to take on this role.

Children are brilliant at holding discussions with each other, arguing their positions, listening, considering and responding. However, the conditions where they can do this best tend to be those where teachers are not present, or at least where children feel they are not being judged to by the teacher. It is possible that the most fluent discussions between pupils are those which are brought to a swift close by the teacher because they are not about the lesson. Sometimes the mere presence of the teacher can limit a pupil's ability and confidence to take part in a discussion, particularly if they have become used to highly teacher-led culture. Some possible teething problems for whole-class discussions around classroom practices might be:

- Teachers find pupils continually waiting for the teacher's prompt for discussion to continue;
- Looking to the teacher for approval of their comments;
- Reluctance to ask each other questions that they really want to know the answers to;
- Discussion dominated by a confident few;
- Discussion lacks momentum and energy; or
- There is very little consensus or agreement.

Whilst some of these issues might sort themselves out naturally through practice, it is worth considering some basic questions about what is going on. Do the pupils understand the purpose of the discussion? Is it clear who is going to make the decision and how that decision will be made following the discussion? Does everybody feel they have a right to participate, and feel that their views count? Do they have the skills of asking questions in front of others?

Here are the approaches that some teachers have found helpful:

- Sit in a circle, with the teacher being part of that circle;
- Discuss what a quality discussion looks like in the classroom and note the features, as a way of evaluating future discussions and evaluating the classes progress in holding quality discussions;
- Ask two or three pupils (and/or a teaching assistant) to monitor which people are asking questions or giving comments, and invite the class to suggest ways for the discussion to be more inclusive;
- Video the discussion and then watch back with the class;
- Practise discussions in smaller groups on topics about their own lives that they all feel they could talk about, e.g., my experiences of, and ideas for packed lunches, or home-school journeys;
- Find non-verbal ways of participating for those who find it difficult to articulate their ideas or questions in words, for example, having hand signals or cards that could be used to express the following: 'can you say more about that please', 'please slow down', 'I like that comment', 'I don't agree with that' and so forth.

Problem-solving

Problem-solving can be something you do in class meetings, but there are also times when problem-solving needs to happen *right now*. You may already have developed your own ways of structuring a problem-solve, but here is a typical example:

Ask:

- 'What's the problem?'
- 'What can we do?'
- 'Which option will we try?'

Try it. Now ask:

- 'Did this solution work?'
- If yes, 'How can we prevent this problem happening again?'
- If no, 'What can we try now?'

(Adapted from Fletcher, 2015)

The informal plenary

This is when the teacher throws a question out to the class to make decisions about the next part of the lesson: 'How's it going?' 'How much more time do people need on this?' Although responses are made individually, these decisions affect everybody in the class.

One of the teachers in my study, Philip, explained that he stops frequently to ask the class how the lesson is going for them. Although he does this to gauge whether his pace and explanations are working for them, he suspects that sometimes pupils just copy the response of others around them, and he is not certain that pupils always give an honest response. Some pupils have had it engrained into them that nobody but the teacher controls the use of time and resources in a lesson, so it may take some creativity to undo this habit and get them participating. However, my participants managed to do this with 10-year-olds, so take comfort from their experience.

Voting

Carl tried to weave CDM into the curriculum as opportunities arose, and his class came to accept not only that they might be involved in making decisions with their teacher, but that they could also initiate this CDM. Having introduced the idea that he wanted his class of eight-year-olds to take part in decision-making, Carl introduced them to some simple voting techniques and encouraged them to discuss when and where voting should take place. See 'Voting about voting' below.

The late David Gribble described a consensus approach to CDM that is more sophisticated than the sometimes crude 'for or against' voting (Gribble, 2015). He described this as introducing a kind of 'graded opposition' to any proposal.

- Supportive disagreement: I don't agree, but I'll go along with it and even help to make it happen;

- Unsupportive disagreement: I won't interfere, but I won't raise a finger to help you; and

- The block: I don't agree and I feel so strongly about it that I will continue to attempt to prevent this action (and maybe even leave the group if it goes ahead).

Although I have never seen this in use, it does seem to enable people to express themselves more fully than a simple yes/no vote.

Voting about voting

Carls pupils liked the idea that they could propose a vote but, he hadn't predicted what would happen next: not only did they sometimes call for a vote themselves, but they started discussing the whole process. They liked the democracy. Even in subjects as trivial as 'doing the votes', they would argue about whether it was going to be a blind vote or if they were going to see how others were voting. Carl could see that they really enjoyed these debates and he got great pleasure from seeing them become more skilled and confident in their arguments.

The pupils started discussing the issue they were voting for, recognising that if, for example, they were voting for some kind of a reward they might feel they had to vote with their friends. They discussed situations where they were likely to be swayed by peer pressure if a vote was public.

Debates about whether to vote blind or not were made with growing confidence: they started to 'call it' for themselves. If they wanted to make an honest vote, but they felt that if people saw them they'd have to vote the other way, they'd take a vote on whether or not it was going to be a blind ballot.

They really liked the idea that they could propose a vote themselves, made up new, fun ways of voting and started debating whether a vote should be preceded by discussion or not.

Randomly selected decision-makers

Not all children need to be included in every decision for it to be collaborative. Research suggests that when pupils know that other pupils like them have been involved in the design of school rules, for example, they are more likely to respect

---

Odd and even

In order to make CDM fun and random, two pupils volunteer to be 'decision-makers' and both pick up a card, laid face-down, from the teacher's desk. The one with the odd-numbered card gets to make the decision.

Research participant Carl's way of helping pupils to gain confidence in CDM.

them than when they believe they have been designed by adults. Participant Carl devised Odd and Even' as a way to help children to have the confidence to make decisions on behalf of their classmates.

Students-as-researchers

Encouraging pupils to act as researchers into their own and fellow pupils' experiences is a great way to get data about pupil perceptions of their schools and classrooms, and ideas for improvement. There is not room here to go into the details of setting up such research, but there is guidance online for those who wish to pursue it (Fielding, 2001; Fielding & Bragg, 2003; Morgan & Porter, 2011). As this book is about collaboration, I propose that pupils and teachers become part of a *collaborative* research team, each contributing to the design and enactment of research into teaching and learning, environment, discipline and so forth, to enable participatory exploration and design to take place (Martens, Meeuwissen, Dolmans, Bovill, & Könings, 2019;).

Opportunistic CDM

Sometimes teachers find unexpected opportunities for CDM, and sometimes CDM just happens. The more it becomes a part of the school and classroom culture, the less conscious teachers may be that they are even using it.

The next story is an example of CDM being included in a plan made by two teachers for a school trip. Nadia was a teacher and fellow doctoral researcher with me at the Institute of Education. We had been talking about my research study just prior to the time this story took place.

STORY: A COLLABORATIVE SCHOOL TRIP

Year 6 teacher Nadia and her colleague Joseph were planning to take their two classes (58 10- and 11-year-olds) on a Maths Trail to explore one of London's most historic streets between Westminster to Trafalgar Square, stopping off to explore landmarks and solving some predetermined maths problems as they went. On the way they had to look out for four sets of things: dates and times and other uses of number; estimation opportunities; shapes; and Roman numerals.

The trail covered the kind of area where as a tourist you could spend two days exploring. The teachers realised that, in reality, there was too much to see for the amount of time the group were going to spend there; if they were going to do the trail well, they would have to have a good ratio of adults to children, so that they were not 'traipsing children around in great packs' in a small and busy space. They invited extra parents along to allow children to be in 12 groups of five, as this would enable them to stop and explore things they found interesting.

Nadia really didn't know how the pupils all did it, but somehow each group decided where they were going to go, in which order and how long they were going to stay there. But what came out of that was that they got to make the decisions. Nadia said that this plan was not their usual one for a school visit: when they do a school visit they usually plan the route, the order of stopping points, how long each stop will last and so on. What was unusual about this visit was that the pupils led the decision-making. Some stopped at a red phone box because they wanted to take their picture inside. Another group discovered a really good view of 10 Downing Street through the arch between the Foreign Office and the Commonwealth Office. Two groups ran into each other, but that was quite rare.

When Nadia and Joseph set this up, they said they wanted their pupils to explore London in separate groups and be a bit independent, because they were going to be in secondary school the following term and needed to be trusted to lead the way sometimes. As Nadia described it, 'Not like little sheep traipsing after an adult.' Nadia and Joseph were concerned that when the pupils arrived at places like St James's Park that there were dangers there. They could have instructed the groups about exactly what to do at these junctures, but had agreed that each group had decisions to make for themselves; they wanted the groups to be very separate and independent.

So, in order to avoid overcrowding as they arrived at different places with their worksheets to look at dates or the height of things (remember, it was a Maths Trail), these teachers had a choice: a) either to let the pupils choose how to do the trail themselves, or b) make up separate routes for 12 groups of children walking around a very small space, then spend most of the visit monitoring and policing the groups to check they stuck to the plan.

Thus, collaborative decision-making came about almost as a 'needs must'– they would have to get the pupils to plan for themselves. The alternative would probably have involved Nadia and Joseph taking three evenings planning all the possible combinations of groups and locations. Nadia told me: 'That is just madness. And then all I'd be is frustrated because be walking around with my group on my going fast enough on my very clear teacher-designed route. I'd be worried that this group is not where they are supposed to be and that group hasn't moved on in time.'

They did a risk assessment and everything went ahead.

Not all the groups visited every location on the trail. What the children found interesting was not the same as what the teachers had thought they *would* be interested in. The children took a wide variety of photographs and wrote about their learning and visit in the school newsletter.

Positive outcomes

- It was a manageable and genuinely enjoyable experience for all involved;
- Different groups focused on very different features of the resource available (the environment of the trail);
- Groups generally had their own space and there was no overcrowding;
- The teachers did not have to spend their time checking that every group was 'where they should be' or 'following the timetable';
- The pupils had time to be engrossed in whatever interested them;

- Although the teachers didn't observe the mechanics of this, pupils appeared to be able to make group decisions about where to go and how long to stay there;
- The parent helpers were freed up from chivvying and 'shepherding' the children from place to place; and
- The children felt trusted and behaved accordingly – there was no silliness reported, unlike previous trips.

Lessons learnt

- You don't have to start out thinking of collaborating with your pupils – it sometimes just comes about naturally when you are planning the best learning experience!
- Groups of five children seemed a good size for this kind of group decision-making; and
- CDM can be one element as part of a wider plan.

Ideas to consider

- The next time you plan a visit, see how loosely you can make the plan, to enable the pupils to shape the experience;
- Be aware of your own planning generally, and try to leave room for pupils to negotiate the timing, order and duration of activities.

Digital technologies

These days, we cannot ignore the great impact that digital technologies have made on systems of communication. The use of digital communication can modernise the collaboration process, and can be used to prepare or follow up on class discussions and other meetings between pupils and staff members. Some pupils and teachers may be able to express themselves more fully using digital technology than face-to-face, and this can empower pupils and staff to bring about changes in the school environment (Rudd, Colligan, & Naik, 2006). I hesitate to list any particular examples, as it is likely that by the time you are reading this book technologies will have moved on and this section will be already out of date. However, as pupils often have expertise and experience in the use of technologies that outstrips that of teachers, collaboration here is essential.

Trust, risk and collaboration

The final three stories in this chapter, Pupils in the Kitchen, Free to Travel and Piano Permission, show how it is possible to pass over some decision-making power and increase freedom of pupils to make their own decisions, whilst managing risk. The stories are worth including because they illustrate some important principles of CDM: the best learning includes some risk-taking; pupils need to feel trusted in order to take risks with their own learning; learning how to manage risks is an important skill; and risk assessment should be used in order to make it safer for pupils to learn through a wider range of activities, not to prevent these activities from happening.

STORY: PUPILS IN THE KITCHEN

School catering manager Hugh MacLennan, inspired by TV chef Jamie Oliver's drive to improve school dinners, thought that the best way to do this would be to get pupils involved in food preparation (BBC Press Office, 2007). At that time, the school had a growing number of pupils from Eastern Europe, many of whom came from families who were themselves in the catering trade. So he approached the head teacher and together they made a plan for pupils to be able to use a school kitchen to make breakfast for the many pupils who arrived at school early, many of whom would not have had breakfast before leaving home.

Once the collaboration between pupils and kitchen staff took off, pupils started to treat the school kitchen as their own, and would book sessions to make birthday cakes for their friends and families. The catering staff trained up volunteer pupils to use the kitchen equipment, follow hygiene rules and prepare breakfast for themselves and fellow pupils. Every day, pupils were involved in all aspects of the working of the school kitchen, and on occasions, such as the Christmas lunch, pupils devised the menu and prepared the food.

Whilst others might be put off by health and safety requirements and risk assessments, Hugh's head teacher backed him 100 per cent, saying, 'Where's there's a will there's a way.' They both agreed that knowledge of food is an important life skill, and felt that, from a health and safety viewpoint, there should be no reason to treat it differently from physical education lessons or technology, or other potentially hazardous skills on the curriculum. Their risk assessments led to a kitchen induction programme and food hygiene training being added to the curriculum, as well as ensuring that there was a safe ration of staff to pupils in the kitchen, particularly during busy times. There were certainly times when Hugh and his fellow kitchen staff wondered why they had taken this on, but with full commitment of catering staff to the initiative, they felt it was worth the effort.

Positive outcomes

- Pupils developed a really good knowledge of and relationship with food;
- The educational potential of the school kitchen and kitchen staff was realised; and
- Pupils who may not have been achieving previously gained valuable culinary skills.

Lessons learnt

- A single member of staff with a strong vision can make a big difference to staff–pupil collaboration;
- Pupils are willing to put in time and effort to learn new skills when they see this as a gateway to new opportunities;

- Strong commitment from senior leaders is essential, as is having a highly trained staff who share a collaborative ethos;

- A positive approach to risk management plans can help schools to enrich the curriculum; and

- By starting small (breakfasts only to start with) the initiative was manageable.

Ideas to consider

- Assess which school resources (catering, maintenance and administrative facilities and people) could be more fully exploited for educational purposes;

- Teach risk assessment to pupils so that they can be involved in collaborative risk assessment when planning new ventures – particularly useful as pupils see risks that adults fail to pick up, such as what nine-year-olds may be tempted to do in a given situation; and

- Staff session on risk assessment to explore ways of seeing collaboration as a risk-reducing exercise (if pupils can use kitchen equipment safely and are handling food more hygienically, the risk to their future health and safety is reduced).

STORY: FREE TO TRAVEL

I was attending an Annual Review meeting for a nine-year-old boy at a special needs school. At the end of the review, the teacher leading the meeting asked the boy to show her the colour of his badge. When she saw that it was yellow, she told him that he could find his own way back to class.

At lunchtime I noticed that each pupil was wearing a badge in one of five colours. The teacher at my table explained that they had designed an 'independent travel' programme so that pupils could be as independent as possible and still be safe. The way the programme worked was this: a pupil who could not yet safely and reliably move from one room to another in the same building was given a blue badge. This meant that if a member of staff or other pupil saw a 'blue badge' pupil walking around the school unsupervised, that something had gone wrong and they would need to be accompanied back to class. The next colour was awarded to those pupils who were safe to move both within and between buildings on their own, and the next one was for pupils who could also safely walk to the bus stop outside the grounds. Beyond that, colours signified freedom to walk to the local shop, and the ultimate was to be deemed safe to walk around the nearby town in pairs or small groups. All pupils were working towards their next zone of travel and given opportunities to test out the skills for the next stage. There were procedures in place for the very rare pupil found crossing the boundaries of the next stage.

Positive outcomes

- This arrangement gave greater freedom to staff and pupils;
- Staff spent less time accompanying pupils around the school who didn't need it;
- Pupils said it felt good to be trusted to walk around without an adult at their side;

- Visitors, local shopkeepers, bus drivers and parents understood when pupils were outside their safety zone during lunch time, for example;
- Not all pupils had to be treated the same way in terms of freedom to move about independently; and
- Pupils were proud of their rising independence and very rarely overstepped their travel limits.

Lessons learnt

- Although this story might not seem immediately relevant to CDM, what it does illustrate is that there may be stages to collaboration and that decision-making can be built into the school system. A system that is transparent allows pupils, parents and staff to challenge judgements made for any given pupil, and is seen as fair and caring. The decision-making in this story is the decision about which colour or level of safety was appropriate.

Ideas to consider

- Ask pupils and staff to identify aspects of school policies and procedures that treat pupils, or staff, as if they were unsafe and untrustworthy, and discuss how trust could be extended whilst keeping people safe; and
- Ask yourself, if we really trusted all pupils (and staff, parents, visitors) what would it look like?

STORY: PIANO PERMISSION

Derry Hannam, retired democratic teacher and schools inspector, was on a visit to a well-known democratic school in the United States. The pupil who was showing him round led him into the well-appointed music room and Derry spotted a grand piano. Being a keen jazz pianist, he sat down and opened the lid to have a play. The pupil immediately asked him to stop, saying that nobody was allowed to play the piano without first being 'certified'. He explained that to be 'certified' you had to show that you knew how to play the piano. Each department was looked after by a 'corporation' of staff and pupils with a special interest or expertise in that particular area. Accordingly, any use of the instruments in the music department was governed by the music corporation. 'Who could give me this certification?' asked Derry. 'I can. Play me something you love.' the boy replied. So Derry played for him and, having convinced the boy that he knew how to play the piano, he was duly certified (Meighan & Harber, 2007).

Positive outcomes

- The pupil had a sense of ownership over school property;
- A valuable instrument was well cared for; and
- Derry got to play the piano!

Lessons learnt

- Pupils can take care of valuable school property if this is entrusted to them; and
- Pupils are capable of interacting with adults as equals, and with authority.

Ideas to consider

- List items of valuable school equipment and discuss with pupils how they might help to look after these items;
- Identify damage done to school property over the past year, accidentally or otherwise, and collaborate with pupils to find ways of preventing such damage in future.

References

BBC Press Office. (2007). Former restaurant chef's return to school leads to Radio 4 Food & Farming Award. Retrieved May 7, 2015, from http://www.bbc.co.uk/pressoffice/pressreleases/stories/2007/11_november/28/food.shtml

Brough, C. J. (2012). Implementing the democratic principles and practices of student-centred curriculum integration in primary schools. *Curriculum Journal, 23*(3), 345–369.

Cox, S., & Robinson-Pant, A. (2008). Power, participation and decision making in the primary classroom: Children as action researchers. *Educational Action Research, 16*(4), 457-468

Fielding, M. (2001). Students as radical agents of change. *Journal of Educational Change, 2*(2), 123–141.

Fielding, M., & Bragg, S. (2003). *Students as researchers: Making a difference. Consulting pupils about teaching and learning.* Cambridge, UK: Pearson Publishing.

Fletcher, A. F. C. (2015). Tips for Teachers: Meaningful Student Involvment Everyday. Retrieved March 3, 2020, from soundout.org

Gribble, D. (2015). Democratic Decision-making. Retrieved December 2, 2019, from https://www.davidgribble.co.uk/index.php/democratic-decision-making

Martens, S. E., Meeuwissen, S. N. E., Dolmans, D. H. J. M., Bovill, C., &Könings, K. D. (2019). Student participation in the design of learning and teaching: Disentangling the terminology and approaches. *Medical Teacher, 41*(10), 1203–1205.

Meighan, R., & Harber, C. (2007). *A sociology of educating.* London: Continuum.

Morgan, B., & Porter, A. (2011). Student researchers exploring teaching and learning: Processes and issues. In G. Czerniawski, &W. Kidd. (Eds.), *The student voice handbook: Bridging the academic/practitioner divide.* Bingley, UK: Emerald.

Rowe, G. (2018) Democracy in the primary classroom. Unpublished thesis. UCL Institute of Education. Retrieved from: www.pupilparticipation.co.uk/resources

Rudd, T., Colligan, F., & Naik, R. (2006). *Learner voice: A handbook from futurelab.* Bristol, UK: English Secondary Students Association (ESSA).

6

Negotiating the curriculum

Teachers are always under pressure to design and deliver the perfect curriculum and assess its impact almost before the ink has had time to dry, and you know you've got it right when you witness the engagement and productivity of your pupils. Wouldn't it be amazing if you could find a way of designing lessons that took less preparation and made it much more likely that your pupils would invest more of their own energy and effort into lessons? Although this might require a new approach to planning, wouldn't it be worth it?

Australian educator Garth Boomer defined curriculum negotiation as 'deliberately planning to invite students to contribute to, and to modify, the educational program, so that they will have a real investment both in the learning journey and in the outcomes' (Boomer, 1992). Negotiation of the curriculum gives all pupils ways to develop and practice autonomy and control, needs frequently unsatisfied in the school setting (Glasser & Gough, 1987). Designing something for a lesson or course really makes pupils feel worthwhile and wanted.

Negotiating the curriculum with pupils involves two sets of decisions: content and delivery (or process); *what* they are to learn and *how* they are going to learn it. This chapter tackles each of these in turn. I will first say something about consultation.

Consulting pupils

Consultation about the curriculum involves teachers asking pupils for their opinions or ideas about teaching and learning. It can sometimes be a first step towards CDM. However, if the teachers, having heard what pupils have to say, then make the actual decision themselves, it falls short of CDM.

In the extensive studies on consulting with pupils about teaching and learning carried out by the (Economic and Social Research Council) ESRC in the early 2000s, secondary school pupils were asked to comment on teaching and learning approaches they had experienced in their schools. Teachers were then invited to take up the pupils' suggestions, and the research found positive reported impacts on both teachers and pupils. Interestingly, one of the conclusions of this study was that rather than pupils being invited to talk *about* teachers, teaching and learning, they need to be talking *with* teachers about teaching and learning. It is only through such dialogue that pupil voice takes his rightful place in collaboration (Fielding & Rudduck, 2002).

Transforming consultation into CDM

Quite often when consultation is used, rather than CDM, it is because factors such as time, cost and policy requirements need to be taken into account. The teacher may indeed be the only one who can make the decision, but often, if the teacher shares with the pupils the additional information that will impact on the decision, the pupils can collaborate more fully. For example, if cost is a limiting factor to deciding which type of bookshelves to buy, pupils may offer to fundraise, or volunteer a family member who could make the shelves for less money if they are made aware of the budget. If the teacher is concerned that the decisions around the length and timing of break-times may disrupt other classes, discuss this with the class and make the decision openly, together. If other members of staff need to be consulted, involve the pupils in this discussion, so that they experience the nature of negotiation, and appreciate the constraints their teachers are working under – and maybe offer suggestions about how to overcome these constraints or even help with strategies to help their teachers to increase their freedom to make their own decisions, in partnership with their pupils, about classroom issues.

A 2018 study shows how two schools used a survey to consult with pupils, but where the first school stopped at consultation, the second school went on to involve pupils more fully in decision-making.

The first school wanted to make sure that they were buying books that the children would want to read. They used a Google survey to find out:

- children's reading interests;
- how much reading they did; and
- whether they liked talking about reading.

In the second school, teachers used SurveyMonkey with pupils to find out how they liked to learn, and used this in their planning. Through this survey, they found that pupils wanted to have more of a say in the order they did things during the day.

- the teachers discussed the survey results with the pupils;
- the pupils designed a provisional timetable for the day; and
- this new timetable was trialled and discussed.

Although no great changes were made, the pupils loved doing it and it felt like they had chosen the way they were going to work, rather than having it imposed on them (Mayes, Finneran, & Black, 2018).

Negotiating curriculum content

Typically, schools do not have complete freedom to design their own curriculum. Exam boards define what is to be examined and government education departments around the world define, in varying degrees, their respective national curriculum requirements. However, rather than being a limitation to negotiating the curriculum with pupils, it can be helpful to have an existing structure within which to make collaborative decisions.

Ways in which teachers have tackled this include:

- Using the four questions in the table below as a class exercise;
- Getting pupils to volunteer to be on planning groups;
- Giving the syllabus for an exam to some pupils who have nearly completed the content, and ask that they put this into pupils-friendly language for pupil who have yet to begin the course of study;
- Involving pupils in discussion of the purpose and meaning of the syllabus and what it might contain; and
- Inviting the class to come up with reasons why the syllabus content might be useful or interesting things to learn.

The stories later in this chapter, *Girls' PE Curriculum* and *Making Sense of Maths* are examples of how two teachers collaborated in curriculum decision-making involving consultation and negotiation. Both the teachers in these examples had curricular demands placed on them that they could not themselves negotiate, and yet they were able to negotiate with their pupils within these boundaries.

When there is no prescribed curriculum, teachers are free to negotiate both curriculum content and process. Professor James Beane, a former teacher, devised a 10-step framework for teachers to use when negotiating a curriculum with their pupils. I include an abbreviated version below to illustrate an approach which, whilst having great value, may be a pipe dream for teachers in state schools who have to work within the boundaries of a National Curriculum. Many home educators have found Beane's approach to be an effective and stimulating model. Recent research

---

The four questions for a new course of study:

- What do we know already? (What don't I need to teach them about);
- What do we want/need to find out? (What questions pupils have; what they don't know; what they are curious about);
- How will we go about this? (You might want to say how you usually teach this course, and invite pupils to help you to redesign it; agree timescale and order; find out who has specialist knowledge of this topic); and
- How will we know, and show, when we have finished? (What we have found out; what new skills we have acquired; our future plans).

(Adapted from Boomer, 1992)

Ask pupils:

- What questions do you have about yourself, e.g., Does my heart beat when I sleep? What is dandruff?
- If you or other children are joining in, are any of your questions similar?
- Think of as many questions you have about the world around you, e.g., What are the bubbles on our pond? What's the brown in dead leaves?

Are there any common themes, e.g., Reflex Actions, Nature's Chemistry? Which questions could be covered under each theme?
Jointly suggest ideas for activities. You have a curriculum!

(Adapted from Beane, 2005)

tested this model in five secondary schools in the Netherlands and Belgium, countries where teachers have greater curricular freedom than in UK schools. Although the experience of using this model was not without its difficulties, and required high levels of skill from teachers, one of the study's main findings was that pupils put most effort into tasks they had designed themselves (Bron, Bovill, &Veugelers, 2016).

STORY: GIRLS' PE CURRICULUM

Forty-one 15- to 19-year-old girls from an urban secondary school took part in a research study around negotiating the PE curriculum with their teacher (Enright & O'Sullivan, 2016). The girls needed guidance and encouragement, but rose to the challenge and took ownership of their learning. Although these girls were already being offered a 'girl-friendly' PE curriculum, it had been conceived and designed by adults and was very much teacher-led, even though research around 'girls' views of PE' had informed the design. The team for the study involved the researcher, Eimar, the PE teacher, Mary, and five student-researchers. The study involved three phases: naming inequities; broadening horizons; and change-agency.

Naming inequities (six weeks)

The team designed a Task Book to find out the girls' general interests, teach them some research methods, and encourage self-reflection about physical activity and suggestions for the PE curriculum. Focus groups used these books and additional information from Physical Activity Logs kept by the girls to come up with ideas for PE activities and highlight what influenced the girls' enjoyment or non-enjoyment of physical activity.

Broadening horizons (10 weeks)

The girls chose activities they would like to try, and taster sessions were taught by the PE teacher or outsourced if they did not have the expertise. The girls mainly chose individual and non-competitive activities, e.g., gym, dance, Boxercise, rock climbing, Pilates, and aerobics. Pupils liked the idea of any exercise they could do to music.

The pupils took on different roles within the lessons (peer-teachers, timekeepers and attendance monitors, warm-up leaders, disc jockey, etc.). They experimented with a range of assessment methods such as self-scoring, teacher-graded work, poster presentations, written assignments and group discussion. Protected end-of-lesson time enabled the girls to 'talk back' about that day's PE lesson.

The questions from these sessions (sometimes facilitated through discussion and questioning, and sometimes through discussion of questions on posters) could be used in any subject, and covered the purpose, outcomes and process of a lesson. They also reflected on what helped them to learn, and how learning could be evidenced.

Through a focus group, pupils discussed their involvement in decision-making in school and, specifically, in PE. They decided which aspects of the curriculum they would like to be more involved in: register; warm-ups; choice, location and order of activity; playlists; rules and assignments.

Interestingly, the girls acknowledged that there were some non-negotiables such as appropriate kit, safety rules, mandatory curriculum requirements and listening to teachers 'because they are listening to us'.

Change-agency

Through a series of curriculum design sessions, the five student-researchers worked with their PE teacher to co-construct an eight-week curriculum based on all the information gathered so far from pupils and grounded in their expressed interests and motivations.

When asked what this project was all about, the girls agreed the following: to think about and try new things in PE that will help us to *like* being active; help us to be active *more*; and they anticipated that 'it will all be good fun.' Whilst Mary was pleased with the positive response of most pupils, a couple didn't care as much as the others and one girl saw the whole project as a way for the teacher to shirk her responsibility: 'That should be your job, shouldn't it. So what are you going to be doing, if we're doing your job?' (Enright & O'Sullivan, 2016, p. 213).

The girls started to become much more eager to participate in PE and were coming to school with the right kit. Invited to reflect on the new curriculum, the girls were clear what had changed. There was more discussion and roles assigned to those who forgot their PE kit, e.g., session DJ, or warm-up leader. Girls who used to forget their kit were now bringing it, as they felt they had picked the activities, so they may as well do them. They loved being in charge of the music and picking their own playlist. They had used an approach called *Photovoice* (Wang & Burris, 1997), which involved taking photographs of activities for later discussion, and this went down very well, and even their attitude towards written tasks had changed: 'We'll even do writing sometimes and we won't be moaning 'cos its ours.'

The girls really engaged in the new activities they had chosen – which included climbing, badminton, aerobics and dance – and they enjoyed the discussions and leadership opportunities.

As might be expected, pupils were much more likely to listen and respond to encouragement and prompting from their peers than from teachers, but they also gained a greater respect for what it takes to be a teacher – it was harder than some of them thought!

Everybody involved acknowledged that the new curriculum was more meaningful and relevant than any PE curriculum they had previously come across. The girls were able to see the value of their own prior learning, interests and experience, and this gave the PE curriculum more meaning in their lives. *They* owned it, it was *their* curriculum.

Positive outcomes

- Co-construction of the curriculum meant that a 'we chose it, so we do it' culture developed;
- Girls who had previously avoided taking part in PE started enjoying lessons;
- The teacher learned a lot about the girls' lives;
- New PE activities were introduced into the school, broadening options for all current and future pupils;
- The pupils gained a greater respect for what it takes to be a teacher;
- The girls were able to see the value of their own prior learning, interests and experience, and this gave the PE curriculum more meaning in their lives; and
- *They* owned it, it was *their* curriculum – I know I've said this already, but it's such a powerful message that I can't help repeating it.

Lessons learnt

- A curriculum devised collaboratively will be more meaningful and socially relevant for pupils;
- When a small group of pupils take on the role of researchers, other pupils co-operate and value the outcomes;
- Focus groups, activity logs and *Photovoice* can be useful tools for finding out about pupils' experiences and ideas;
- Sometimes outside expertise is needed;
- Don't assume pupils are aware of all the options; and
- Pupils are more likely to listen and respond to encouragement and prompting from their peers than from teachers.

Ideas to consider

- Use focus groups and activity logs to generate useful data for curriculum design and also provide a baseline for assessing impact of the curriculum;
- Keep an Activity Log of a specific activity, e.g. reading carried out by your class, and use to discuss how school-based reading could be made more relevant to pupils' experience and interests;
- Sometimes work with a sub-group of pupils to make discussions manageable;
- Be open to involvement of people who are not on the school staff;
- Get pupils to take photos of lessons for reflective discussions; and
- Have Class 1 exchange their photos with Class 2, discuss each other's' photos and exchange reflections.

STORY: MAKING SENSE OF MATHS

Maths teacher Susan, aware that her pupils had experienced seven years of being told how to learn, decided to negotiate the maths curriculum with her mixed-ability class of 12-year-old pupils in order to develop the best conditions for learning. There was a small group of teachers in her secondary school who were doing similar things with their classes. These teachers planned to spend the first few lessons at the start of the school year in class discussions about their subject, what was going to be learnt and how they would go about learning it.

Putting collaboration into classroom culture

Using an approach that involves pupils supporting, challenging and cooperating with each other requires that they get along with each other and are able to respect and trust each other. However, Susan's pupils were used to maths classrooms where they worked in silence or maybe helped people sitting next to them from time to time. She had to design ways to encourage pupils to help each other and discuss mathematics together without the need for teacher intervention. Susan did this by:

■ Making it clear that it was appropriate for pupils to get up and walk around to seek or offer help;

■ Inviting a couple of pupils to help her to respond to others who had their hands up for help; and

■ Asking pupils to spend one lesson a week helping a classmate.

In order to make sure that pupils were helping each other in the right way, especially as they had little practice in doing this in their previous classes, Susan organised class discussions about the best way to help each other. It was clear, as weeks went by, that pupils really appreciated help from their peers, finding it more useful in many ways than help from the teacher. They also started to appreciate the benefits reaped by those doing the explaining, in terms of the depth of their own learning and the ability to explain what they knew to somebody else.

Teaching strategies

Susan's teaching was based on learning as an active process, building on and adapting the learners existing knowledge and vocabulary in the light of new information. Following the negotiation model, Susan's lessons combined a range of following strategies:

■ Brainstorming;

■ Class discussion;

■ Group discussion;

■ Pupils as audience for writing and presentations; and

■ Pupils as developers of tasks and resources for others to use in their learning.

A common concern that some teachers have about negotiating the curriculum with their pupils is that there are some facts and rules the pupils just need to be told, and that they will never learn these if they are given a say in what and how they learn. Susan saw no incompatibility between memorising a method or a formula and her approach. Rather, she had seen that when pupils really understood a concept, they found it easier to remember these things. Susan described that this understanding of mathematical concepts was nurtured when:

■ She allowed herself and her pupils allow enough time to develop class and group discussion skills;
■ Pupils learned to share their ideas and ask each other questions;
■ Every pupil felt safe in the knowledge that all their contributions would be valued;
■ She became more skilled in timing these discussions so that they didn't interfere with pupils' flow of concentration;
■ She learned how to respond to incorrect pupil explanations in a way that helped them to self-correct without telling them that they were wrong; and
■ She avoided using any guess-what's-in-my-head style teaching.

Occasionally, Susan would give a mathematics class a 'writing lesson' to deepen pupils' understanding of the concepts they had been learning. The lessons went like this:

■ Pupils agree which concept or method, that they have been working on, to discuss;
■ They brainstorm what they know about this;
■ They discuss in groups what they might write about it;
■ The groups report back to the class;
■ The class discuss the writing and then work in groups to write their own definitions.

By the end of these lessons, pupils would have done a lot of thinking, working out, talking and writing about mathematics. Through these processes, they started to make much more sense of what they had been learning. Susan discovered that one of the most powerful outcomes from these writing lessons was that pupils were writing *for themselves*. They started to see that writing was a tool for learning, not just something they did for their teacher.

Pupils as textbook authors

Susan encouraged pupils to 'write mathematics' for each other. She would give groups of pupils parts of the text to rewrite so that it was easier to understand. She found that this was a great way to help them to be articulate the language of mathematics, and to practice different ways of explaining the same concept.

When Susan's mathematics class rewrote the exercises, they sometimes adapted what was in the textbook and sometimes rejected the textbook's accounts in favour of their own explanations and examples. Once Susan had checked a group's textbook rewrite, the group would present their work to the class and take on the role of teacher as they set tasks and answered questions from the class.

Pupils learned to negotiate:

■ Skipping exercises if they already felt confident with that type of problem; and
■ Asking for extra, or easier, exercises if they felt the need for more practice

Covering the curriculum

Most of Susan's colleagues in the maths department were *not* negotiating the curriculum with their pupils, so after two terms she was able to compare the amount of work covered after working in this way, with that covered by her colleagues. She was delighted to find that not only had they covered the same amount of work as the other classes, but that pupils across the ability range had found the experience enjoyable and satisfying. Not only had they learnt the maths, but they had learnt many skills relating to their own learning and learning as a community. They were also able to write about and articulate their learning.

Susan was surprised at how good the pupils' judgements were about their own needs, and it made her realise that in her former teacher-led approach there must have been many pupils who were either bored or anxious in lessons that had been planned without their involvement.

Pupils who finished their work early were invited to help Susan to select the next topic for the class to study. Over time, pupils became adept at planning their own individual topic work; working in a group to plan a topic for others; or working in a group of friends to plan topics for their own group.

Previously, Susan had determined the order in which topics would be taught to the class. Because the class had a maths book, some pupils simply kept to the sequence of topics given in the book. However, they learned to adapt the sequence depending on what they did or didn't know already, or were or weren't interested in.

Within the class of young teenagers who had little or no prior experience of taking part in the design of their curriculum, some found the transition really hard. Some set unrealistic tasks for themselves and then felt a sense of failure when they could not complete them. Others lacked confidence in their own ability and set tasks that were undemanding, particularly those who were trying to avoid repeating the failure they had experienced in previous mathematics classes.

The work that Susan had to do to develop pupils' confidence, self-assessment and self-direction required her to nurture a relationship of trust between herself and her pupils. Helping pupils to start to develop responsibility for their own decisions around what and how much to learn, sometimes involved helping them to deal with confrontation and disillusionment as well as co-operation and friendship.

Part of Susan's skill was knowing when to give pupils a rest from decision-making, and when to keep encouraging them to keep trying with their decision-making. Throughout this process, Susan involved her pupils in discussions about what was going on for them in this new negotiated decision-making, and allowed them to express some strong feelings about this. Some pupils were really pleased to have this opportunity involved in decisions about how they learn and genuinely surprised at being allowed to do so. However:

- Others were suspicious of their teacher's intentions;
- Some of them felt that there must be some manipulation going on, and needed to see that the teacher was serious about giving them a say before they relaxed and accepted her approach; and
- Some pupils lacked the confidence or imagination to see themselves as being able to learn without being told what to do all the time, and so felt dismayed.

Susan developed an approach to each of the less positive responses:

Suspicious pupils need:

- Time to make up their own minds;
- Their teachers to give reasons for their instructions;
- Their teachers to ask how they are going about their learning; and
- Their teachers to avoid giving improvement suggestions (this can be interpreted as a direction that needs to be followed, as this is students' past experience of some teachers)

Dismayed pupils need:

- More attention and guidance until they become more confident in themselves;
- Help to trust their existing knowledge and judgements about new subjects;
- The teacher to discuss their interests and experience with them;
- A limited set of alternatives to help them to learn to make choices from a list of options, before they generate their own; and
- Teacher attention and encouragement to overcome their prior experience of failure and low confidence.

Pupils showing contempt need:

- The teacher to avoid falling into a similar negativity as theirs;
- Their negative statements to be confronted; and
- Reasonable persuasion.

(Adapted from Hyde, 1992)

Positive outcome

- By learning to negotiate, pupils avoided spending time on unnecessary exercises and were able to help Susan to make sure that the level of challenge of the work was appropriate for all pupils;
- Some pupils were really pleased to have this opportunity to collaborate with their teacher, and this transformed their perception of both the teacher and the subject;
- Pupils learned how to use the language of maths and became skilled at finding different ways to explain the same concept;
- Compared to other classes in the school not using collaboration, Susan's class not only covered the same amount of work in two terms, but pupils across the ability range had found the experience enjoyable and satisfying;

- Pupils became skilled in writing and talking about their learning; and
- Not only had they learnt the maths, but they had learnt many skills relating to their own learning and learning as a community.

Lessons learnt

- If pupils have little or no prior experience of taking part in the design of their curriculum, they may set unrealistic tasks for themselves or set tasks that are undemanding, particularly those who are trying to avoid repeating the failure they may have experienced in previous mathematics classes;
- A teacher needs to know when to give pupils a respite from decision-making, and when to keep encouraging them to keep trying with it;
- Some pupils who have been deemed successful under conventional assessments may resist collaboration, worried that they might not do so well by other approaches;
- If you are a teacher using non-authoritarian teaching methods in an authoritarian school, be prepared for strong pressures to conform. Be prepared to build bridges with colleagues who may be disapproving or fearful; and
- On reflection, Susan felt she initially rushed into sharing power in her classroom. As she became more experienced, she developed collaborative strategies in a much more measured way, building skills and trust more carefully so that it would come as no surprise when she started to invite pupils to share power in the classroom. Her classrooms became much more ordered and systematic than when she first started negotiating the curriculum.

Things you could try:

- If you get some less positive responses, don't be surprised – this is new for them too – but try out Susan's responses when you encounter them.

Negotiating curriculum delivery

Even teachers who can see how pupils could be more involved in negotiating *what* they will learn may struggle with the concept of involving pupils in decisions about *how* they will learn. And yet, I observe many teachers doing just this without realising that they are using collaboration or negotiation. Conversely, I have observed many lessons where teachers offer no opportunity for pupils to shape the lesson, even when they are not learning anything from it.

A few years ago, I led a Students-as-Researchers project in a London secondary school (Rowe, 2015). As part of their research, students interviewed teachers to find out about their most enjoyable teaching experiences. Overwhelmingly, the teachers reported that the most enjoyable and fulfilling lessons were those where pupils came up with something unexpected which enhanced or changed the direction of the lesson – often including humour – or where pupils provided suggestions or ideas the teachers had not thought about themselves. It was enlightening for students, and for me, to hear teachers say that their best experiences involved unplanned pupil input, which they found far more rewarding than pupils simply following instructions, working hard and completing tasks. It is interesting to note that not only did the teachers and pupils in this study enjoy the interview experience, but the pupil researchers also described how they started to see their teachers as fellow human beings, who they had more in common with than they had thought previously.

Science teacher, Charles Eick took the opportunity to get groups of pupils together to make decisions with him about aspects of his curriculum process. First, he drew up a list of all the curriculum processes he wanted to collaborate with them on, and invited his pupils to form committees to develop each area. For each of these areas he defined the outcomes needed. These areas included: homework criteria; assessment methods; rules and procedures for classroom functioning; guidelines on late work and making up for missed assignments; components of a 'good' science class; and safety guidelines. The pupil groups each came up with a consensus on a set of proposals around Charles' outcomes, which he then negotiated with the class. Charles was pleased with the outcomes. For example, the final, agreed, homework policy included the following: Homework only on Tuesdays and Thursdays, no weekend or holiday homework and no tests on Mondays. All homework will be linked to the topic being studied and no 'meaningless' worksheets, definitions, book work and word searches. Charles found that the cooperation and productivity of his pupils relied on his readiness to collaborate with them: 'I came to realize that, as teachers, we often structure our classes in ways that work against our students' success. My pupils were attempting to restructure some of the business of the classroom to help them be more successful learners' (Eick, 2001).

Primary school teacher Carl, the first participant in my doctoral study (Rowe, 2018), explained to his class that he had no choice but to follow the National Curriculum, and that this left limited room for him to negotiate the curriculum outcomes with his pupils. Carl's approach to curriculum planning was to have a number of different possible lessons in his head rather than *one* lesson that he was determined to deliver in *one* way: 'I plan very loosely so it's very easy for them to take on, to let them shape the lesson.'

STORY: JUNGLE BOOK

Carl's Year Five class (9- to 10-year-olds) had been studying *The Jungle Book*, and his pupils asked if they could make Jungle Book masks. He agreed and they made the masks during the Art lesson. Following this, the pupils kept asking if they could use the masks in Drama to do a performance of *The Jungle Book*. Carl agreed, and took the opportunity to weave in aspects of the curriculum that he knew needed covering. He managed to tailor it so that they looked at direct speech and drama, at using a script rather than direct speech and what the differences were, and then they did the play with their masks on.

Carl became as immersed in the play as the children were, and was delighted to discover how much of the curriculum they covered without his having to make specific lesson plans for everything.

STORY: LANDSCAPE VS. PORTRAIT

In a Maths lesson on co-ordinates that I observed, the pupils had been given instructions to work in pairs to draw a table on which to record their results. After a few minutes a pupil, Sanjit, approached Carl and suggested that the table would fit better on the page if they turned it sideways and completed it in landscape view instead of portrait. Carl said, 'That's a good idea, why don't you suggest it?' Sanjit turned to the class with an air of confidence, tucked the book under his arm and, in imitation of his teacher, clapped a rhythm to attract the attention of his classmates. They looked up and clapped the customary response. Sanjit offered his suggestion; they stopped what they were doing to listen; and many of them took up his idea. Although Sanjit seemed confident, having had his idea validated by Carl, it was still good to see the beam on his face when other pupils told him what a good idea it was.

I observed how this interjection from a pupil seemed to have a focusing and energising effect on the class, and Carl told me that he had noticed this happening when pupils, rather than the teacher, gave advice or suggestions.

Lessons learnt

Carl found that the more he allowed pupils to shape the curriculum, the more creative they were and the more energy they put into the work. Pupils had little reverence for subject boundaries, and were just as happy to suggest a drawing task in a maths lesson as they were introducing science into an English lesson. Sometimes Carl would invite them to make decisions with him, but as Carl's collaborative ethos took root, pupils felt free to offer suggestions and show initiative.

Carl felt that through CDM, his pupils were learning that the adult doesn't always have the best ideas. He said that being involved in decision-making was fun for pupils and often led to additional learning outcomes that he hadn't expected.

Planning a maths lesson together

In one secondary school, a teacher and his pupils planned a maths lessons together. Instead of preparing the worksheets as he had previously done, this teacher invited pupils to help him to plan a lesson on angles. One of the pupils designed an activity where pupils had to write down their initials in bubble writing, draw several lines across the letters and then use a protractor to mark the angles. Another pupil suggested that they could then colour them in and stick them up on the display. (Mayes et al., 2018)

This example illustrates how, when owned by the pupils, even a dry academic task can be transformed into something that is seen as *fun*. In my experience, pupils have a natural tendency to design tasks that are inclusive, as in the example above. Pupils who lack confidence might stall when given the task of measuring and recording angles on a worksheet. These same pupils may well feel able to attempt a bubble letter and some line drawing without the need for additional adult support. Consider also the reduction on the teacher's workload (and school budget) by removing the preparation and printing of 30 worksheets.

Other approaches that teachers have used include pupils in the following ways:

- Designing and delivering 'recap' lessons at the end of a module of work;
- Researching a topic and delivering a lesson on that topic;
- Involved in selecting themes for the week and planning activities; and
- Generating challenges they can complete as a class.

A new planning

In the many years I have been paying attention to teacher–pupil collaboration, I've been struck by how frequently the changes suggested by pupils match those their teachers had in mind, 'how' to make it read or when they are given a say in restructuring the curriculum or timetable, there appears to be no great change. I've some comments to make on this.

Firstly, if the pupils have had a hand in designing the curriculum or timetable, then although an observer might see no great difference, there is a massive difference in the way pupils now view the curriculum: it now belongs to them!

Secondly, we have to accept that children and adults become institutionalised and may not consider radical alternatives to what they have already experienced. This is where the development of an Educational Imagination can be helpful. More will be said about this in Chapter 8.

Earlier in this chapter, I described how one of my research participants, Carl, developed a mantra of: 'plan loosely so that pupils can shape the lesson'. My second participant, Michael, also found that CDM required a new approach to planning, which he referred to as 'planning for unpredictability'. Participant number three, Philip, described his best lessons as those where he made a plan, but adapted it through the lesson using a set of 'mini-plenaries'.

A teacher who had been in one of my CDM workshops contacted me to tell me how she had changed her planning strategy as a result of considering how she could involve her pupils more in CDM. She was about to plan a lesson on 'difficult words' where she would help pupils to distinguish between homophones, or remember non-regular spellings, for example. Instead of making a list of the words they would cover in the lesson, she decided to ask the class to identify which words they struggled with. She was surprised to find that these were not necessarily the words she would have identified. However, she based the lesson around their list, and reported to me that pupils had been the most productive and co-operative that she had ever seen them. She put this down to their involvement in the planning of the lesson content, and said that rather than involving any extra planning, the planning had been done by pupils through this simple act of collaboration.

References

Beane, J. A. (2005). *A reason to teach: Creating classrooms of dignity and hope.* Portsmouth, NH: Heinemann.

Boomer, G. (1992). Negotiating the curriculum. In G. Boomer, N. Lester, C. Onore and J. Cook (Eds), *Negotiating the curriculum: Education for the 21st Century* (pp. 4–13). London: Falmer.

Bron, J., Bovill, C., & Veugelers, W. (2016). Students experiencing and developing democratic citizenship through curriculum negotiation: The relevance of Garth Boomer's approach. *Curriculum Perspectives, 36*(1), 1–30.

Eick, C. (2001). The Democratic scienceclassroom: science teaching that can improve student behavior and enhance inquiry. *Science Scope, 25*(3), 27–31.

Enright, E., &O'Sullivan, M. (2016). "Can I do it in my pyjamas?" Negotiating a physical education curriculum with teenage girls. *European Physical Education Review, 16*(3), 203–222.

Fielding, M., & Rudduck, J. (2002). The Transformative Potential of Student Voice: Confronting the power issues. Paper Presented at the Annual Conference of the British Educational Research Association, University of Exeter, *England, 12-14 September 2002. Consultation, Community and Democratic Tradition Symposium.*

Glasser, W., & Gough, P. B. (1987). The Key to Improving Schools: An interview with William Glasser. *The Phi Delta Kappan, 68*(9), 656–662.

Hyde, S. (1992). Sharing power in the classroom. In G. Boomer, C. Onore, N. Lester, & J. Cook. (Eds.), *Negotiating the curriculum: Educating for the 21st century* (pp. 67–77). Abingdon, UK: Routledge Falmer.

Mayes, E., Finneran, R., & Black, R. (2018). Victorian Student Representative Council (VicSRC) Primary School Engagement (PSE) Evaluation Final Evaluation report PSE. Melbourne.

Rowe, G. (2015) Students as Researchers into their own Classroom Climate: How appreciative inquiry changes perceptions. Unpublished report. UCL Institute of Education. Retrieved from: www.pupilparticipation.co.uk/resources

Rowe, G. (2018) Democracy in the primary classroom. Unpublished thesis. UCL Institute of Education. Retrieved from: www.pupilparticipation.co.uk/resources

Wang, C., & Burris, M. (1997). Photovoice: Concept, methodology and use for participatory needs assessment. *Health Education and Behaviour, 24*(369–87).

7

Culture and leadership

This chapter identifies two priority considerations for collaboration to thrive in a school: culture and leadership, both of which have a powerful impact on the attitude towards, and readiness for CDM.

What is school culture, and why is it important for CDM?

Sometimes called 'school ethos', a school's culture can be described as 'the way we do things here'. A school's culture consists of assumptions, values and beliefs and the way that these are reflected in behaviour and policies, and impacts on everything that happens in a school. And yet how often does the school culture appear as an agenda item the senior leaders or staff discussion?

It is just as important for school leaders to keep an eye on the school culture as it is for farmers and sailors to monitor the weather. When leaders are clear about the school culture they want, they can communicate it to others, and are able to review aspects of school culture which need attention. This enables them to reflect on school policies and practices with reference to the desired culture, and to determine what might need to change.

School culture influences everything else

Pupils arrive at this school early to set out equipment for the day's work, make breakfast and coffee for teachers and fellow pupils and set up clubs of their own to develop skills and help other pupils who were struggling with work. Pupils get down to work as soon as they are ready, and do not have to wait until the slowest pupil is ready. It is almost as common to see a pupil talking to the whole class as it is to see a teacher doing this. On joining the school, younger pupils are taught by the older pupils how to care for each other and their classroom. Pupils can apply to take part in training programmes run by school support staff in office administration (including stock taking, money handling and banking, photocopier maintenance, ordering, telephony, organisation of publicity for school events), building maintenance (including paintwork, gardening, heating systems, furniture maintenance, path cleaning and gritting) and catering (including hygiene, portion control, budgeting, presentation, food preparation, maintenance and safe operation of equipment). Following successful completion of these programmes, the pupils can apply to hold a responsibility based on their skill competence. Staff and pupils can relax or carry out their planning and homework together in several areas throughout the school. There are frequent discussions which involve both pupils and staff about how to improve the quality of aspects of school functioning.

Where is this school? How did they achieve this? I have yet to come across such a school. And yet a growing number of school leaders are investing time to discuss and plan the kind of culture where these things could happen.

All schools develop a culture of one sort or another; some are designed, and some are accidental. We know from Organisational Psychology that unless deliberate care and attention is paid to it, a school culture will develop that may not be the one you want. Teachers are likely to struggle to introduce a culture of cooperation and collaboration in their classrooms if they are working within a non-collaborative culture. Although most of the positive aspects of participation in a school come down to the attitudes and beliefs of individual teachers, head teachers and pupils, *how* those characteristics show themselves can be strongly influenced by school culture.

Researcher Steve Wilson found that whilst relatively few aspects of the conventional school culture support collaboration between teachers and pupils, there are many more cultural elements that actively *inhibit* it (Wilson, 2002). Wilson found that teachers and pupils who are most ready to collaborate with each other all possess a strong desire to be involved in change, a belief in the right to participate, and the ability to keep going in the face of difficulties. The strongest personal feature of teachers who had strong participatory practices was that they held what Wilson called 'celebratory perspectives of youth' (p. 90). That is, they had positive perspectives towards young people and would support them in personal projects outside the classroom as well as encouraging pupil-innovated projects. Wilson concludes that for participation to thrive, pupils and teachers need to be given the scaffolding by school leaders to develop the skills and opportunities to take part in decisions concerning school development.

Lack of teacher voice featured as a common inhibitor to collaboration. Teachers in teachers in Wilson's study also felt that the written school policies on participation were there 'for show', and they as teachers felt continually 'under the microscope' from inspectors, parents and others, which made it safer to maintain conventional authoritarian roles than involve pupils in decision-making. Teachers described how they had come to adopt an 'accountability mentality' that was at odds with participation and felt they had to go 'cap in hand' to the head when they wanted to make a decision. Teachers were held back from involving pupils in curriculum design by an understanding that curriculum was the 'province of the professional' and that pupils lacked the motivation and skills to participate in decision-making

Researcher Audrey Friedman studied the ways that collaborative (democratic) teachers cope in schools where they themselves have little say about what goes on (Friedman, Galligan, Albano, & O'Connor, 2009). Her team identified four subcultures:

- compliance – going along with school practices but feeling powerless, devalued and incompetent;
- noncompliance – these teachers also feel devalued and lacking in autonomy but refuse to implement new school practices, even though these may be good for pupils;
- subversion – teachers appear to comply but maintain their own democratic classrooms practices, which they may keep to themselves; and
- democratic inquiry and practice – teachers openly challenge new initiatives that they feel are not in their pupils' best interests and collaborate with colleagues and are open to having their own practices scrutinised.

All except the last subculture have negative implications for teachers, pupils and school management. But don't lose hope; all of these negative subcultures can be avoided if a whole-school culture of collaboration is adopted.

The collaborative school culture

The collaborative culture is one where traditions, policies, processes and established practices reflect collaboration; decision-making will be visible, participative and open to challenge. The style of leadership will be distributive; whilst school leaders maintain an overview, steer the direction of change and accept ultimate responsibility, this is done in partnership with staff and pupils.

School climate

The easiest way to identify a school's culture is to examine the school *climate*. The climate of a school is 'the way it feels' and can be felt differently by different people. Where a school culture may take months or years to address, school climate is something that is more changeable, and measures of climate are snapshots of a school or classroom, a kind of temperature-taking. Do people feel safe, included, able to be themselves and express their ideas, or does the school culture leave some feeling judged, isolated and powerless? Both culture and climate set the tone for how things happen in the school. To find out what a schools' climate is like, you have to ask those who spend time there.

The environment

Another way to tell how collaborative a school is involves taking a look at the classroom and school when the pupils are not around. Does what you see signal collaboration or not? Research has shown that the environment has the power to both reflect and shape behaviour and attitudes. Unless we are aware of the messages that people get from the environment, we can unwittingly create a school or classroom which gives a message about learning and behaviour which is not the one we intend (Daniels, 1989).

For example, one sign that collaboration, or at least a child-centred orientation, is present is the height and content of wall displays. One teacher told me that she had involved her six-year-old pupils in decisions about which learning aids they would like on the classroom wall and where these should be placed. The children told her that they wanted a number line to help them with their counting and would like to write and colour in the numbers themselves. They decided that the number line be placed at chest height so that they could run their fingers along the numbers, as they counted.

Melanie, who had recently taken over as head teacher of a primary school, observed that there were lots of notices around the school: 'shut all windows before leaving'; 'leave these toilets as you would wish to find them'; 'clean sink after use'; 'don't run'; 'no pupils to use this door'. She discussed these signs with the staff, who agreed that they conveyed the message that pupils and staff were unruly, dirty, careless people who needed to be told and reminded what to do – and they all agreed to take these signs down.

What messages do your displays give about collaboration?

- 'We produce great work together'
- 'We don't have to work on our own – we help each other'
- 'Pupils own this space'
- 'This is for pupils to look at and enjoy and learn from'
- 'Anybody can suggest ideas for display'

Collaborative leadership

An important feature of the collaborative school is that head teachers and senior leaders will encourage decisions to be made, wherever possible, by those most affected by them. In a local primary school, teachers feel free to get together to solve problems and to develop and design new practices. For example, teachers in one year group recently agreed a flexible break time between their three classes, to give them more control and flexibility over their own timetables and use of shared space. The teachers felt able to make this decision between them, since they felt trusted, and their decision did not impact on other staff. The teacher who described this to me said that it was a really satisfying experience to work with her peers in this way: "It was a huge relief to be able to take a small stress out of our school day."

One school I know of has a junior leadership team (JLT). At the end of school assemblies, the head teacher and JLT stand at the front and the head teacher invites questions or comments from anyone in the school. This can be a question or comment from the youngest pupil or the most experienced teacher, and are all given equal respect and consideration. If it appears that some action is required that could be carried out by pupils themselves, the head teacher turns to the JLT and asks them if this is something they could handle (which they usually can). This arrangement:

- gives all children the confidence to ask questions or make a comment in a large group of people, safe from the fear of ridicule;
- helps pupils feel trusted to carry out tasks often given to members of staff; and
- reduces the workload of the head teacher and her staff.

What a collaborative school culture looks like

In schools where CDM becomes a way of life, certain things will be happening:

Environment: Attention is paid to aspects of physical environment of school (toilets, recycling, gardens, etc.; school food) that facilitate collaboration and/or are designed by those who use it. For example, dining arrangements will be designed with pupil and teacher input and be attractive places for pupils and teachers to dine together; pupils help identify black spots for litter or bullying and help identify, design and implement environmental changes needed to solve these problems.

Curriculum planning: Teachers and pupils are involved in class discussions on curriculum content and lesson design. In this way pupils hear from teachers about aspects of teaching and learning that they would not otherwise have thought about, and vice versa. The curriculum builds on pupils' interests and experience. Pupils and teachers have the opportunity to bring their own ideas of what they enjoy into school.

Policies: Principles and processes around homework and discipline, for example, are jointly devised. In the place of punishment, there is discussion and joint decision-making about conduct, both for teachers and pupils. Skills for community problem-solving are taught and practiced using real-life situations as they arise in the school and classroom. Pupils and teachers collaboratively generate and evaluate solutions for social problems in their own schools and classrooms.

Shared Roles: Pupils take on roles previously carried out by adults. There are more shared activities, where pupils and teachers can learn about each other and discover what they have in common. For example, pupils and staff meet together to plan parents' evenings, sports day and other events.

Decision-making: Skills for discussion and decision-making are explicitly taught to pupils. Training and regular updates are given on ways to broaden collaboration in the school. Staff and pupils attend training as equal participants.

Free from fear of failure: The whole school adopts a collaborative culture. Instead of looking for people to blame when mistakes are made, or thinking up excuses when things go wrong, people openly seek help from each other and are not ashamed to admit that they are not perfect.

Imagine what it would be like if your school had all of the above in place.

Leadership for CDM

Greetings, school leaders! If you've got this far in the book I'd like to think you're either already running a collaborative school or you are seriously thinking about it. Either way, three things will help you to succeed with collaborative decision-making in your school: fellowship from other professionals to give you courage to embark on what is still new territory for many schools around the world; information from research with others who have already trodden this path; and an outline of a plan.

A friend recently asked me what my book was about. After a few minutes of conversation, where I described the idea of teachers sharing decision-making with their pupils, she said, 'I don't want to sound rude, but it's not exactly rocket science is it? Why aren't all teachers doing that?' I have to admit that before I carried out my own research I had similar thoughts, and it was only through a close and extended contact with teachers who were using CDM in their own classrooms that I started to understand the many factors that make it hard to teach in this way. First and foremost, I learnt that you will find it difficult to sustain this way of teaching for any length of time unless it is explicitly made a priority throughout the school. Secondly, for pupil voice to thrive, teachers and other staff must themselves have a voice. All participants in my own study (Rowe, 2018) had head teachers who were highly supportive of their use of CDM, voicing approval privately and encouraging them to carry on teaching in this way. Positive recognition from the head teachers was highly valued by participants but at the same time they felt that their head teachers, who had little personal experience of teacher–pupil collaboration themselves, were not well-equipped to either advise them when they were stuck, nor confident to raise the use of CDM in staff forums, however positive they felt when they observed it happening in the classroom. So I would say that a third condition is for school leaders to be well-informed about what a collaborative culture looks like, and to develop a plan for developing and sustaining this in their own school.

In the past, explanations for poor achievement of disadvantaged pupils sometimes pathologised the families and looked for factors outside the school for these inequalities. School leaders who are serious about addressing inequality of pupil outcomes monitor their own school practices and processes to ensure that these are not contributing to or exacerbating disadvantage. Once school leaders recognise their own school culture is not a neutral factor, they can start to reduce the way that the school itself might maintain and nurture social inequalities.

The teachers in my research told me that although they had developed CDM in their own classrooms, nobody had ever suggested that they teach in this way during their training or in their professional supervision. They had rarely come across other examples of CDM, and there was little in their own schools' cultures that overtly encouraged, promoted or supported the kind of CDM they were attempting to develop with pupils. CDM needs to be modelled by school leaders – are you prepared to change your own approaches so that collaboration is central to the way you lead and manage in your school?

There is no single method or approach to starting up CDM in a school, but I have studied reports from head teachers, researchers and others to find out what some school leaders have found useful. As you will see, the main leadership role is to lead others to create that culture which enables *teachers*[1] to generate ideas for involving pupils in decision-making, not in generating the ideas themselves. It takes patience and persistence to bring CDM into a classroom – even for teachers who have a strong faith in children's ability to take responsibility for their own decisions – and it

---

1 Although I am a talking about teachers in this book, teaching assistants (paraprofessionals or teachers' aides) and admin staff need to be included in this, as it is essential to have them on board to create your collaborative school culture.

is crucial that this is supported by a whole school approach with active involvement of governors and senior leaders.

Although there is no one way to approach leadership for CDM, the teachers and school leaders I work with said it would be helpful to be given some structure to work from, accepting that this is based on research and reports described above, and has not been tried and tested in this form. The four steps below are based on research and are informed by ideas from psychology about what helps school innovations to get off the ground and be successful.

Step 1: Gathering support

Head teachers are so busy looking after everybody else, but not so great at putting their own needs first. You are embarking on a period of organisational change that is going to be exciting, groundbreaking and fruitful. However, you may be working within an educational system where competition and individual attainment is prized far more highly than collaboration and community, so it's going to be challenging. In choosing to do this you are going against an authoritarian tide and you will meet opposition from both within and outside your school. That's why it's really important to find other like-minded people, a community of practice, from within your own school and beyond, who value collaboration in education and with whom you yourself can collaborate. Make sure that you have at least one other head teacher who wants the same for their school, plus a mentor who understands collaborative decision-making – this could even be a school governor or a parent who works in an organisation (not necessarily a school) with a highly collaborative culture.

The Australian state of Victoria requires all classrooms to take pupil voice into account. A number of these schools now have a well-supported 'facilitating teacher' within the staff who is responsible for pupil voice work. This person has a number of roles:

- Co-ordinating professional development sessions for teachers;
- Ensuring that recommendations from pupils result in action; and
- Making connections with other schools and organisations to keep bringing in fresh ideas.

(Adapted from Mayes, Finneran, & Black, 2018)

Once your pupils are experiencing CDM this person may seek or create opportunities for links with head teachers, teachers and pupils in other schools where CDM is also being introduced or developed.

Step 2: Engaging with your school culture

CDM requires a whole-school approach, but this doesn't mean that everyone has to do the same thing. In fact, conformity is one of the aspects of culture that can make collaboration difficult. Collaboration needs to be a golden thread running through the organisation; a way that people relate to each other and is supported not by a list of rules, but a set of principles, as described earlier in this chapter.

For pupil voice to thrive, teachers must first have a voice themselves. My second participant Michael felt that it is illogical to give children a say in the curriculum unless teachers, who have spent years in training and know their pupils' abilities, are given more of a say in how they run their classrooms. This was backed up by my third participant, Philip, who said that in his school the staff were sometimes consulted, but he was very clear that the senior leadership team made all the decisions.

Barriers to teacher–pupil collaboration

Many teachers have never come across CDM, nor has it been suggested they teach in this way. I know from my own experience and research that there are few examples of classroom CDM around for teachers to use as models, and most will have little or no personal experience of CDM from their own schooldays.

CDM can be contrary to the traditional culture that tells teachers that they must 'control pupils or be controlled by them'. Interviews with the teachers in my study uncovered a constant tension between the natural instinct to control on the one hand and the natural instinct to let go and share decisions on the other. They felt dominated by considerations of time and results, and felt they were putting inadequate time into teaching pupils the skills for decision-making. They also worried that CDM might make them look weak in the eyes of pupils, parents and colleagues.

Putting employees first

It is important that school leaders model CDM with their staff by giving teachers a voice in decisions that affect them. My experience leads me to propose that teacher voice *precedes* pupil voice. A few years ago I heard a programme on the World Service about a businessman called Vineet Nayar who was the CEO of a large company in India. Nayar had turned conventional business thinking on its head by suggesting that instead of putting *customers* first, that the well-being of *employees* should be the employer's priority. He argued that it is from happy and well-motivated employees that customers will get the best service. It shouldn't be surprising then therefore if pupils also receive the best education from teachers and teaching assistants who feel valued, trusted and included in decision-making. There is evidence that teachers who are excluded from decision-making are unlikely to support school initiatives around pupil participation (Fielding, 2001a).

Only when the climate amongst staff enables them to talk, question and complain legitimately about aspects of school life, and not only be consulted but take an active part in decision-making, will they be in a position to start to collaborate with their pupils. Such staff participation might require:

- Restructuring of staff meetings to promote active staff participation in decision making;
- Monitoring who talks most in staff meetings;
- Asking staff:
    - Do you feel valued, listened to, involved in decision-making?
    - How do you feel about how decisions are made in this school?
    - What do you enjoy most about working here?
    - What issues do you want to see on our agenda?

- Planning professional development for staff around issues identified by staff members;
- Ensuring that teaching staff contribute to the School Development Plan;
- Regular, scheduled opportunities for pupils and teachers to come together to discuss, plan and evaluate CDM.

Many of the suggested starting points in Chapter 8, to help teachers to introduce CDM with their pupils, can actually be adapted for school leaders to use with their staff. For example, I have already come across fruitful staff discussions based around the question, 'Which aspects of your work in this school would you like to have more of a say in?'

Step 3: Professional development

The aim of any professional development in CDM is to:

- Raise awareness of CDM;
- Prepare staff for a new relationship with their managers and pupils;
- Motivate staff to participate in designing the school culture;
- Give staff the confidence to start successful collaboration with their pupils;
- Develop a common language of participation and collaboration that can be used to build communication between and amongst pupil and teacher groups; and
- Identify and develop the skills and perspectives needed for CDM.

The type of collaborative discussion that teachers will have with pupils in the classroom needs rehearsing in staff-only groups initially so that they feel at ease with this style of conversation. Once they are clear about the benefits of these types of conversations, they can discuss options for setting up similar conversations with their classes.

In some schools, teachers can end up taking a passive role in staff development sessions and expect the senior leadership team to do all pre-meeting preparation, set the agenda and decide on follow-up actions. If this is so, then the first step is to reorganise these sessions so that authentic discussion, deliberation and debate takes place between staff. In my experience, teachers really enjoy in-depth discussion with each other on issues about learning, teaching, pupils and school practices. They like to be reminded why they came into teaching in the first place and to feel that they are continually developing the quality of their pupils' school and classroom experiences.

For teachers who are not used to such group conversations, it can be helpful to have a structure and focus to begin with. Here are some ideas to get staff talking about collaboration:

- List the assumptions you make about equipment and resources in the school and your classroom. For example, who 'owns' these? What is the annual budget for consumable resources? What do you assume is covered by school contents and public liability insurance?

- In groups of two to three, compare your notes and discuss what other assumptions you might have about distribution and care of resources.
- Discuss which aspects of resource and equipment management already involves staff collaboration and the benefits and drawbacks of this.
- Discuss whether more sharing and collaboration could result in greater access to equipment and reduced costs.
- Come together as a staff and debate both sides of the argument.
- Whether or not an agreement is reached about greater or lesser sharing and collaboration, staff then discuss the process they have just been through; reflect on the discussions; how they felt; the resulting outcomes, e.g., new knowledge, reinforced frustration, new agreements; and decide whether this approach to discussion could be used again in future.
- Head teachers may initially feel uncomfortable being part of group discussions with their teachers, and vice versa, especially if discussions have previously been strongly directed by the head.
- Peer coaching and observation for coaching purposes in each other's classrooms helps to reinforce where collaboration is already happening and identifies opportunities for further collaborative practices.
- Encourage teachers to keep and share journals of ideas and questions around CDM.

Once teachers feel listened to, they will be more likely to engage in professional development around CDM with pupils. If possible, introductory sessions on CDM can be led by teachers who share their experiences of using CDM in the classroom. Awareness-raising sessions might use stories from this book, or excerpts from Chapter 2, Rationale and Psychology, as the basis for group discussions. The professional development will be ongoing, but initially teachers need just enough to understand the concept of CDM, and have reassurance that their early experimentation with CDM is fully supported by their colleagues and managers. This is something that can be done in a staff workshop where teachers identify aspects of collaborative decision-making they have already tried; discuss with others and reflect on how the practices improve both the learners' and teacher's experience; try to understand why the increased participation had this impact; plan ways to build on current practice.

Step 4: Action

If the development of a collaborative culture is to be taken seriously, the school development plan needs to include a 'bold declaration' of the intention to collaborate (MacKay, 2007) . The next step is for the school's participation policy to be developed with input from staff and pupils. Does every teacher (and other school staff) have a range of ideas and activities to help children express their views? Is it a policy that pupils should be listened to? Supported in expressing their views?

A participative school culture is more likely to be embedded and sustained if there is a dedicated team focusing on this aspect of school life. Ideally, this group consists of volunteers from teaching and support staff and pupils. It may be that after an introductory session staff are invited to work in their year groups or faculty to discuss how best to introduce CDM to their pupils. This is where it is useful to have a core CDM team to co-ordinate and communicate the various approaches in the school.

Organisations where people co-operate and collaborate have the healthiest cultures, and teachers may become disillusioned if they feel that 'pupil participation' itself starts to become a competition between teachers. If individuals see themselves as joint authors with colleagues of a school culture, they will be more willing to co-create and pilot new approaches and be open to new ideas from colleagues and pupils alike. While teachers collaborate with their pupils on how to get started, school leaders can focus on developing a whole school culture that supports greater collaborative fellowship amongst staff and between staff and their pupils.

Reluctant teachers

Unsurprisingly, given the hurdles need to be overcome described above, some teachers find it hard to adopt to a new collaborative culture. However, it is not always a bad thing for some teachers to hold back with school innovations. In a large-scale UK study carried out by Cambridge researcher Jean Rudduck and her team, adolescents were consulted about their responses to the teaching and learning approaches they had been exposed to in their schools. When teachers were given information about their pupils' preferences and dislikes for certain classroom practices, some teachers held back in implementing their pupils' suggestions and others made immediate changes to their lessons. Some of those who showed initial reluctance to implement changes actually ended up making sustained changes in line with pupils' suggestions. At the other end of the scale, a couple of teachers who made changes straightaway ended up resorting to their previous way of teaching, as they had overestimated their pupils' ability to take the lead in class learning. It does seem like school leaders could provide a governing hand in the pace of change, recognising which teachers need encouragement to take greater or fewer risks in collaboration.

I once asked the principal who had successfully changed her school culture what proportion of staff needed to be on board with an idea for it to be possible to implement in a school. She said that she reckoned that she could take change forward if she had one-third of staff who were keen on the idea, one-third who would go along with it, and no more than one-third who were reluctant or resistant to change, She then asked me an unexpected question: 'Which of these groups do you think give me the greatest problem?' Although I might have said 'The reluctant ones', I guessed that things might be more complicated than this by the very face with which she asked me this question. Sure enough, she replied that it was the highly enthusiastic teachers who were most problematic. She explained that she had to keep an eye on these teachers because they were the ones likely to form a group together and may lead to the development of two separate factions in the staff: those who supported the change and those who didn't.

When Pedagogy and Curriculum researcher Dr. Eve Mayes gave school principals the chance to give some frank comments about their experiences with staff, they had interesting things to say:

- Some teachers found it hard to do the 'student voice thing';
- Some found it hard to change their way of teaching, particularly the more experienced teachers; and
- Some teachers won't say what they really feel, for fear of being seen as out of step with the principal's proclaimed collaborative ethos.

Another of the school principals felt that sometimes, especially if CDM is in a school's strategic plan, teachers just need to be told that change is now going to happen!

Whilst some might find it uncomfortable for a head teacher to just drive through a policy or culture change, this is a reminder that a collaborative approach means that everything is done to make it possible to contribute to decision-making – it doesn't mean that decisions aren't made or that policies aren't adhered to.

One principal described how they had taken a cautious approach to introducing pupil voice activities:

> 'If you just open the floodgates to that, and children present a challenge to a teacher in a way that feels uncomfortable to the teacher, the teacher will close the doors again'
>
> (Mayes, Finneran, & Black, 2018).

So how can you bring on a new way of viewing pupils in teachers who currently hold traditional views about the roles of teachers and pupils? Research shows that the teachers who are most negative/fearful/reluctant are those who have never experienced collaborative classroom practices in their own school days, and who have never shared decision-making with their own pupils. Conversely, the more experience teachers have of sharing power, the more they evaluate and the more they want to do. With some exceptions, teachers who start to involve pupils more actively in classroom decisions rarely revert to their previous, conventional teacher roles.

- Hold discussions between teachers about their perspectives on collaboration in teaching and learning decisions to identify what stops and teachers from involving pupils in decision-making;
- Encourage teachers and pupils to discuss why they might themselves limit the scope of their own collaboration with each other and how they might overcome these; and
- Find new ways for the school community to share accounts of their collaborative practices, successes and challenges.

References

Daniels, H. (1989). Visual displays as tacit relays of the structure of pedagogic practice. *British Journal of Sociology of Education, 10*(2), 123–140. Retrieved from https://doi.org/10.1080/0142569890100201.

Fielding, M. (2001a). Beyond the rhetoric of student voice: New departures or new constraints in the transformation of 21st century schooling. *Forum, 43*(2), 100–109.

Friedman, A. A., Galligan, H. T., Albano, C. M., & O'Connor, K. (2009). Teacher subcultures of democratic practice amidst the oppression of educational reform. *Journal of Educational Change, 10*(4), 249–276. Retrieved from https://doi.org/10.1007/s10833-008-9090-x.

MacKay, T. (2007). *Achieving the vision: The final research report of the West Dunbartonshire literacy initiative.* Dunbarton: West Dunbartonshire Council

Mayes, E., Finneran, R., & Black, R. (2018). Victorian student representative council (VicSRC) primary school engagement (PSE) evaluation final evaluation report PSE. Melbourne: Victorian Student Representative Council (VicSRC) Retrieved from https://www.academia.edu/41223522/Victorian_Student_Representative_Council_VicSRC_Primary_School_Engagement_PSE_Evaluation_Final_Evaluation_report_PSE_-December_2018

Rowe, G. (2018) Democracy in the primary classroom. Unpublished thesis. UCL Institute of Education. Retrieved from: www.pupilparticipation.co.uk/resources

Wilson, S. (2002). Student participation and school culture: A secondary school case study. *Australian Journal of Education, 46*(1), 79–102. Retrieved from https://doi.org/10.1177/000494410204600107.

8

Teachers and CDM

In this chapter I am going to be talking about the kinds of things that have helped other teachers to bring the pupils in their classes into a more collaborative relationship. If you are not using CDM as part of a whole school culture, an approach where collaboration is encouraged in every aspect of school life, I strongly recommend that you read the section on Lone Teachers the end of this chapter.

What it takes to be a collaborative practitioner

Can all teachers learn to share power? Research suggests that the teachers who have the most reservations about CDM are those who have never experienced such practices in their own school days, or who have not yet had a go themselves. It really does seem that the more experience teachers have of CDM, the more they value it and the more they want to do. With few exceptions, teachers who start to involve pupils more actively in classroom decisions rarely revert to their previous, conventional teacher roles (Davies, Williams, Yamashita, & Man-hing, 2005).

Readers might be forgiven for thinking that it is the younger, newly qualified teachers who are most keen on involving pupils in decision-making, and indeed when I have run training events for newly qualified teachers, they tell me that CDM fits in very well with the way they want to teach. However, in my experience many highly experienced teachers also us CDM, sometimes keeping themselves to themselves regarding their practices, aware of the difficulties of discussing pedagogy with colleagues. When I talk about CDM with these teachers, they often seem relieved to realise that there is some recognition for what to them feels an obvious approach.

I have been asked whether there was anything special about the teachers in my study (Rowe, 2018) that might explain why they were already using CDM with their pupils. Head teachers in particular want to know whether *all* teachers can learn to share power with their pupils, or whether this is just for a certain type of teacher. Although certain characteristics have been identified as being present in teachers who independently use more collaborative ways of teaching, such as a belief in children's creativity and a wish to participate, the *culture* of the school is likely to be one of the

Characteristics of teachers in my study who were already using some CDM:

- a positive view about children and their abilities;
  the wish to be their authentic selves in the classroom;
- a willingness to share information about themselves with children;
  open about their own weaknesses and mistakes;
- a strong interest in the lives of their pupils;
- an appreciation of the need for classroom belonging, self-worth, freedom and fun;
- readiness to adapt plans in the light of new information;
  comfortable trying new things;
- patient with themselves and pupils while they learn to collaborate; and able to resist the pressure to conform to traditional expectations.

strongest determinants of how easily teachers will adapt to more collaborative approaches. CDM requires a different kind of teacher–pupil relationship to conventional, more autocratic teaching, and the whole school culture is crucial in supporting teachers to collaborate with pupils. The school culture, discussed in Chapter 7, makes it more or less likely that CDM will flourish.

Teachers who share power with their pupils tends to have a positive view of children and adolescents, and can see the possibilities within them for learning and community building. One Australian researcher, Steve Wilson, identified that the teachers who naturally want to share power with their pupils have a 'celebratory perspective of youth'. Wilson identified a characteristic described as 'wanting in', that is, having 'a strong desire to be involved in change', a belief in the right to participate, and 'the tenacity to persist in the face of difficulties'. It was a few pupils and teachers with this characteristic who were responsible for driving the few positive aspects of participatory culture in the study (Wilson, 2002).

Are you ready for change?

Having had a chance to read the experiences of other teachers and reflect on some of the benefits they and their pupils reap from CDM, and the lessons we can learn from these teachers, it's your turn. Even if you're well supported by a whole school approach and encouragement from your managers to experiment with greater participation in the classroom, it's only natural that you will have some concerns. You have probably had experience over many years of numerous innovations and initiatives and may be wondering, 'Is this just another fad, another approach to add to everything else?'

What would it take for you to feel comfortable asking pupils to help you make decisions about curriculum, solve a discipline problem or improve the quality of your teaching? Could you see yourself stopping a lesson, as Ava did (see *Lesson from Slovenia* in Chapter 4), to discuss with the class what's going wrong? What might stop you from taking a pupil seriously when they say of one of your decisions, 'but that's not fair', as happened to Carl (see Corey's computer time in Chapter 1)? Can you see CDM becoming a way of life for you and your pupils?

Once you start to share decision-making with your pupils, you will enter that wonderful world where, instead of your pupils responding to your questions, you are responding to theirs. Instead of you having to decide how to set the challenge of work at the correct level for each child, they will be guiding you. You will have all experienced this at some time, and I have certainly noticed that in classes where the teacher seems the most relaxed and happy, the pupils seem better at making decisions. It's not always clear which came first, the happy teacher or the CDM. I'll let you judge that for yourselves.

We know, from studying the stories of those who have already used collaborative decision-making in the classroom, something about what it takes to teach in this way. Although head teachers and teachers may be enthusiastic about the idea of collaboration, time spent with the participants in my study exposed me to the reality of the culture, skills and attitudes needed for this to be successful. On a personal basis, the teachers' beliefs about children, head teachers' beliefs about teachers and children's beliefs about themselves and each other are important for collaboration: do you value the views and opinions of your pupils? Are you ready to relinquish some of your current practices? To learn some new skills? To share some of your power with your pupils? To model collaboration covertly in your day-to-day work? (Shier, 2006)

Through such questioning, the likely barriers to be overcome in your own practice or policies start to become evident.

A celebratory perspective of youth

Research suggests that those teachers to whom collaboration comes most naturally hold what Professor of Education Steve Wilson called 'celebratory perspectives of youth.' We may not all start out with this, and maybe your school culture is one where it is considered okay to talk about some pupils in derogatory terms. However, the way pupils are referred to is of great importance if you want to become collaborators in planning and learning (Wilson, 2002). It must be clear from the positive and hopeful way that practitioners talk about pupils that they really believe in *all* pupils, not just the well-behaved studious ones, and think of them as future leaders and carers. Many years ago, I was at a conference where a teacher from Finland showed us a video of his maths lesson. At the start of the lesson, he greeted the class, making a small bow to them as he did so. In the discussion that followed the video, somebody asked him about this gesture. He told us that he bows as a sign of respect to the children in recognition that they are our future politicians, teachers, farmers, doctors and leaders. He said that, even more importantly, they may well be the people who will be looking after him and caring for him in his old age. He wanted to remind himself of the importance of these individuals, and to model respect for them right now, as children.

Our own experiences can be radically shaped by how we view others and treat them. This is not just the stuff of fairy tales, but is borne out by research in Psychology. There is a well-known study in Organisational Psychology, carried out in the 1960s that relates to the way managers' beliefs and attitudes drive their management style.

Professor Douglas McGregor studied approaches to managing people in a range of organisations, including schools, and found people in authority could be differentiated by two very different sets of assumptions they held about people. He called these assumptions Theory X and Theory Y. Theory X Managers believe that employees are naturally lazy, will avoid work if possible, do not co-operate unless coerced and desire security above all. Holding these beliefs, Theory X managers will use authoritarian approaches and coercion, believing that employees need to be directed, coerced, controlled and bribed, and decisions made without involving the individuals concerned. Goals are imposed and rewards are used to control people's behaviour. People who are managed under Theory X tend to behave as expected: they avoid responsibility; require external incentives to apply themselves; and use blame and excuses to avoid the sanctions which are usually feature of Theory X management.

In contrast, the management style associated with Theory Y leads to *higher* motivation and *greater* realisation of both individual and organisational goals. Theory Y managers believe in co-operation and collaboration and avoid authoritarian approaches. This is because Theory Y managers assume that employees are naturally inclined to enjoy work. They believe that the more that people see work as voluntary, the more satisfying it will be; employees will exercise self-regulation when they are doing something they really believe in and have committed to themselves; and will willingly seek responsibility, unless they have had a bad experience of this in the past.

CDM is very much in line with Theory Y style of management, which requires teachers to hold positive beliefs about their pupils' intrinsic qualities. However, many traditional school management systems are based on Theory X assumptions, where pupils just get used to being told what to do by teachers, and school rules are accompanied by lists of rewards and sanctions or 'consequences' that are in reality just a set of thinly disguised methods of coercion, threats and punishment (Glasser, 2000).

Maria Montessori, pioneer of early-years education, reminded us to always look for the good in what children do, and to encourage them to do the same. It is very easy to fall into categorising children negatively, particularly when they have been difficult to teach in the past. Some staff rooms nurture negative talk and practitioners can be drawn into a less 'celebratory perception' without realising it. I remember one day I was in a science lesson, observing as part of a coaching contract. It was a highly practical lesson where pupils collected leaves and cut and pasted them to display the contrasting characteristics including leaf shapes, colours and surfaces. In the coaching session following the lesson I commented to the teacher and teaching assistant on the positive interactions between the pupils and the energy with which they tackled the task. The two of them looked at each other, smiling, and told me that the lesson I had observed was not typical and that I should maybe come back another day to see these pupils 'in their true colours', explaining that this group were normally unco-operative, rude and disorganised in their work. When I tentatively suggested that maybe what we had what I had seen today *were* the pupils' 'true colours', the teacher became quite emotional. She said that she hadn't realised quite how negatively she'd started viewing this class, and that maybe her attitude towards them was colouring their behaviour. Without knowing anything about McGregor, she had reached the same conclusions as he had about the way in which teacher beliefs can influence pupil behaviour. In this example, the presence of a third person had enabled them to step back and view their pupils in a new way. What might help you to do this with your pupils?

The reason I mention this story is to show that beliefs can change. When we start to look for the good in children, for their co-operation, kindness, initiative and attention, that good will grow. As part of the coaching experience, this teacher and teaching assistant decided to start pointing out the positive aspects of their pupils to each other, and to let the pupils know that they had noticed these things. Sure enough, they started to see this class differently, and maybe the class saw themselves and their teachers differently too.

In preparation for introducing CDM, it may be worth spending a few days carrying out an audit of the positive attributes of your groups of pupils, and identifying any negative beliefs you have allowed yourself to started to hold about them that might get in the way of building a collaborative relationship with them – believe me, they may also have allowed themselves to believe some damaging things about you too! What we can learn from McGregor is that when we start to treat pupils as though we believe they are trustworthy, they generally behave in that way. It may take some time for you to help some pupils unlock themselves from negative roles they have taken on, but it is possible – and essential. Teachers participating in Alison Cook-Sather's Teaching and Learning Together project, where pupils and teachers shared their perspectives on classroom life, reported that the study had a strong and positive impact on the way that pupils and teachers viewed each other. They started to see each other as fellow human beings rather than as individuals occupying a role (Cook–Sather, 2007).

A New relationship

In a collaborative classroom, the teacher relates to pupils as fellow human beings whose opinions carry equal value to those of the teacher. This does not mean that they are always right, but that their views are of equal value. The collaborative teacher treats their pupils with as much respect as they would a colleague or adult friend. For without this respect, any expressed intent to collaborate is insincere.

Power is not a zero sum game

Although I have frequently read that teachers are reluctant to share decision-making with pupils because they fear losing control in the classroom, this is not what I hear from teachers themselves. I think that teachers are well aware that they will still be controlling the amount of collaboration in the classroom. I had expected participants in my study to say that they were concerned about being judged by their managers or school inspectors. What I hadn't previously appreciated, though, was the power that the judgement of colleagues held. It seems that on a day-to-day basis teachers may be more concerned about how they are seen by their colleagues than how they are judged by leaders and inspectors. That judgement seems to go along the lines of 'so-and-so is a good teacher because they can really control their pupils' or, in primary schools in particular, that they have 'amazing classroom displays'. The teacher who does *not* spend a couple of days preparing displays before the start of the school year because they are going to collaborate with their pupils in decisions about the layout of the classroom (see *Mrs Fintelman's classroom* in Chapter 4) may come across as 'a lazy teacher' to colleagues who do not understand the philosophy of

CDM. A large-scale UK study into consulting pupils about teaching and learning found that some teachers who, prior to the study, had expressed anxiety about being criticised by their pupils, discovered that this very rarely happened. Instead, teachers found the project brought out the best in both teachers and their pupils (Flutter & Rudduck, 2004).

As I mentioned earlier, researchers have found that it is the teachers who haven't yet tried CDM who are the most anxious about sharing power, and that the more experience teachers have with CDM, the more they want to do it. Before using CDM, teachers sometimes worry that if they don't show pupils who's 'boss' they will lose control and the result will be chaos. For pupils who may already have had years of being told what to do, they certainly need some preparation for a change of culture, or else they may just be confused and uncertain how to respond.

Rather than worrying that sharing decision-making power with pupils will lead to teachers being powerless, we need to remind ourselves that power is not a 'zero sum game', that is, there is not a finite amount of power divided by the number of people that have it. If a teacher chooses to share a given amount of power with pupils, they do not lose an equivalent amount of their own power. On the contrary, what my research suggested was that when a teacher *chooses* to share the power of making decisions, they feel *more* powerful, not less. It almost feels as though the holding onto of power, and the protecting of that power, might actually require more energy than sharing it. Holding onto and using power and control over another person in any relationship can have damaging and sometimes disastrous effects, and the teacher–pupil relationship is no different (Glasser, 1988; Ryan & Deci, 2000).

Start with the pupils, not the curriculum

CDM is a philosophy of teaching and learning, and so it's necessary that your approach starts with your pupils: their experiences, expectations, skills and interests. A pupil may have fascination with wildlife and have learned many things about ecology through their own observations and experiments at home, and yet they may have learnt through previous years of schooling not to expect to use these experiences in the classroom, nor to expect opportunities to demonstrate their skills and knowledge, unless these are in line with the objectives of curriculum that someone else has designed for them to follow. We all know of pupils who may not be doing very well on the school curriculum but who have unusual and exceptional skills and expert knowledge on specific topics: the pupil from a traveller family who knows how to operate and maintain tools and machinery; the young carer with specialist skills in understanding and assisting in feeding and medical procedures; or the pupil with poor school attendance who has helped his grandad to build a shed.

Not all pupils will feel comfortable talking about their interests and opinions, especially when they've had years keeping home life and school life separate. The participants in my study recognised the importance of modelling this kind of personal sharing, and even purposefully showing their own vulnerability, as a way of creating a safe environment in which pupils could talk freely about themselves and their feelings. These teachers had discovered that it was important to talk about their own fears and weaknesses as well as their interests and hobbies, so the pupils would see them as human beings, not some kind of alien teacher species.

I love it when I'm in a classroom and I hear a teacher talking with passion about their own interests. Motivation and passion are contagious. I remember hearing a Geography teacher starting a new topic by telling the class a personal story. He told them that he was really fascinated by coastal erosion, and how, when he was writing his thesis, he camped all around the east coast, taking photographs and making notes about the erosion caused by the North Sea. He showed them on a map where he had been, and pupils immediately started to say which places they had also visited. Some were more interested in talking about camping than the coastal bit, but that didn't matter – he had made a human connection that enabled them to offer something of their own experiences and knowledge to the lesson.

Adapting for different ages and abilities

CDM is not some passing trend, nor is it an approach or technique. It is a whole educational philosophy and is relevant for all pupils irrespective of age, ability and temperament from all socio-economic groups. The stories that run through this book illustrate some of the ways in which this philosophy can be put into practice, but you will need to make adaptations for it to work best with your own particular population. However, some principles apply across all populations:

- There will be always be some negotiable decisions that can be made collaboratively;
- Problem-solving and decision-making skills need to be taught and some need more of this than others especially those from the lowest socio-economic groups; and
- All decision-making in the school will be transparent even when it's is not possible for decisions to be made collaboratively.

For more detail on these and other collaboration principles, see Chapter 7.

Negotiating the non-negotiables

Before you start negotiating with your pupils, you need to be clear about the decisions you are currently making on their behalf, and being clear about which decisions you are not in a position to negotiate on. For example, curriculum outcomes and course content may be imposed on you, whilst certain choices within a syllabus may be up to you or your department. If possible, find ways to communicate these non-negotiables to your pupils, making clear the choices that are open to discussion and negotiation. It may be that you have already made decisions that you either do not want to change or haven't got time to negotiate. In these situations, you can still clarify your own decision-making to pupils: 'We needed to choose a social insect and so Mr Shaw and I chose the Honeybee, since the school has a lot of books on these and Mr Shaw has kept bees himself.'

If the pupils can see the outline of the syllabus that you have to cover, you can start to bring them into discussions such as the order in which topics will be covered and other curriculum decisions outlined earlier in this book.

It is important that pupils learn what to do when negotiation is not available, as it is likely they will find themselves in many non-negotiable situations in the family, school and work settings. I used to worry that pupils from collaborative primary schools might be disadvantaged when they move up to more conventional secondary schools. But in practice, what I found is that, through collaboration, pupils learn how to converse with adults and 'negotiate their own negotiation' in a socially acceptable way.

In Chapter 2, we saw how teaching children and adolescents how to negotiate can help them to feel responsible and gives them what psychologists call a 'sense of agency' – the feeling that they can make a difference to their own lives and those of other people. This sense of agency has been shown to be very important to well-being and mental and physical health. It means that we think we can do something about our own situation, are able to make choices and effect change in our own lives. People who have no sense of agency can end up seeing themselves as powerless victims or see themselves as working towards *other people's* goals rather than their own.

So how does a teacher negotiate the non-negotiables with their class? One way is for the teacher to list the non-negotiables and bringing this list to the class for discussion. The list might contain items such as:

- Everybody must wear school uniform;
- Nobody must interrupt the teacher;
- When the fire alarm goes off everybody must leave the building;
- All children must arrive school for 8:40;

and so on.

A related exercise is to list the assumptions that children make about teachers and each other and the teachers make about children. Sometimes these assumptions get in the way of successful working and good communication. For example, some children assume that because everybody else looks like they are working, that everybody but them knows what they are doing.

There are also some assumptions that teachers make about what is and what is not negotiable. For example, that children should be seated for English and Maths lessons or that the timing of breaks cannot be changed. Once assumptions and non-negotiables are on the table, then a shared understanding can be reached about how change can take place in a way that gives everybody an equal voice.

An educational imagination

In the Preface to this book I invited readers to reflect on the following questions: Why do you want to collaborate with your pupils? How can you bridge the gap with colleagues who are yet to be convinced? And, finally, what are you prepared to change, sacrifice, invest, add, stop or learn in order to make your teaching, leading and policy-making truly collaborative?

There is no doubt that CDM shakes things up – you have to be ready to do things differently, and rethink, or even 'blur', the roles of teacher and pupil (Fielding, 2010). Innovative inventions and significant social changes tend to come about when previously held assumptions have been questioned, such as 'only men can vote', 'a vacuum cleaner has to have a bag', 'all cars engines run on petrol or diesel' or 'a fan needs to have rotating blades'. So why not question some of the assumptions around classrooms: lessons are planned by teachers; children must write every day; children of the same age are taught in the same classroom; homework needs to be set at least twice a week; and so forth.

In a conventional school, decision-making input of the teacher is high. The use of time, selection and management of resources, the content and delivery of the curriculum and rules of conduct are all decided by teachers. Teachers who negotiate have to make radical changes in the way they relate to and respond to pupils. At the same time, there are pressures to conform to teacher norms and possible disapproval from other colleagues. This can create doubt in the minds of teachers. Colleagues who don't recognise the value of pupil talk may complain about the noise level, lack of control and failure to maintain standards. They may also disapprove of the lack of formality in the way that the teacher and pupils communicate with each other. It is important for teachers to discuss their ideas with other teachers both in their own school and elsewhere, as this will help them develop confidence and new ways of responding to pupils.

Indeed, a class could be trained up into discussion and debate by taking a new, collaborative look at some accepted and established school practices that people have previously thought of as unchangeable.

Consider the practice of lining up, for example. In most schools, it is accepted practice that pupils form up in an orderly line before entering or leaving the school building, classroom or changing rooms. It has been an accepted way of controlling pupil movement around the school for centuries. Why not change it?

Reimagining the school and classroom

I was talking to my son about how I might illustrate how things could be different in a collaborative classroom and he liked the idea of some 'starter activities' for teachers to try out and reflect on. He suggested I try to recreate scenarios of lessons I have observed and imagine how these might be different if CDM is taking place. This exercise reminded me of the eminent American sociologist, Charles Wright-Mills. In his 1959 book *The Sociological Imagination*, Wright-Mills described how a discipline such as sociology comes into its own when practitioners take a step back from established practices and try to look at the familiar with new eyes. This re-seeing of the familiar is as valuable today for educators as it was in the 1950s for sociologists, and the rest of this chapter is intended to encourage readers to use their *educational imagination* – to transform yourselves into *educational imaginators*, if you are not there already. (Mills, 1959).

Scenario 1a: Assembly

Classes file in one by one, teachers and TAs reminding children to be quick and quiet and sit in neat class rows. Music has been chosen by a teacher and this is played as they come in and sit down. The teacher whose turn it is to plan an assembly introduces the theme and runs the assembly as a combination of reading a story, asking questions of the children and coming up with a conclusion. This is followed by recognition and awards session where certificates are handed out for work completed or good behaviour, etc. The assembly ends when the teacher has finished and she/he invites each teacher to take their classes back calling them out one at a time.

Q: What evidence of learning does this scenario suggest? What role would teachers have played in this learning? What role would peers have played?

Scenario 1b: Assembly

Children make their way into the hall as they are ready and sit where they want and greet those around them. When all children and their teachers are in, four children walk to the front of the hall and everyone stops chatting, and children ensure that those still chatting stop so that the assembly can begin. The four children at the front have volunteered to give a presentation to the pupils about a project they have been working on, and have brought some models to show everyone. A pupil who they have asked to 'chair' their session introduces the group. They describe the project and invite questions from children and teachers, which they answer. The chairperson fields the questions and keeps an eye on the time. When the allotted time is up, he/she asks if there are any notices for the pupils or staff and ensures these get heard. Pupils can ask questions or give information during this time. For example, if someone has lost something, or wants to ask for information but doesn't know who to go to for the answer, they can ask now. The assembly finishes with a song, and as they are singing pupils start walking back to their own classes. They have the choice to leave early or wait until the song is over, so that the exit doesn't get too crowded. Some older children escort younger ones back to their classrooms.

Q: What evidence of learning does this scenario suggest? What role would teachers have played in this learning? What role would peers have played?

Scenario 2a: Maths lesson

The children in Ed and Sam's class are invited by the teacher to come and sit on the carpet and are told that today they are going to learn about the 24-hour clock. The teacher uses the smart board to demonstrate with images what the 24-hour clock is for, how to read it, and involves some children in answering questions about why people might get confused using just a 12-hour clock. Some children, including Ed, offer their own experience of seeing/using a 24-hour clock when at the airport or for train timetables. Sam says nothing at all. No child questions the teacher, challenges facts, asks for her to repeat what she said or requests further explanation. The class is set the task of translating 12-hour times into 24-hour times and vice versa and putting a list of mixed 'times' into the correct order. This involves cutting out and sticking into their books.

Q: What evidence of learning does this scenario suggest? What role would Ed and Sam's teacher have played in this learning? What role would peers have played?

Scenario 2b: Maths lesson

As the class come in from break, Ed and Sam hand each child a post-it note on which is written either 'play', 'eat', 'sleep', 'school', 'home', 'light', 'dark'. Last week their teacher asked, 'Who already understands what the 24-hour clock is about?' Ed and Sam volunteered to explain what they knew to the class and to think about ways to help others understand time.

Ed and Sam had found a website with a diagram of the 12- and 24-hour clock, alongside which they used to talk about why 24-hour clocks can help in certain situations. They talked about trains and TV programme schedules. They then invited the other pupils to come up and put their sticky notes on the chart on the whiteboard, to say when they would be sleeping, eating, etc., and when it would probably be light or dark. They then did a quick quiz for the class using the chart, 'give a time when you might be eating lunch/sleeping/in school/doing homework/it would be dark/light, etc.'. During the session, many children asked questions or for Ed and Sam to repeat themselves if they were not clear. They also picked them up on some inconsistencies and errors in their presentation. The task the boys set the class was to work together in groups to create a 24-hour clock that could be a day in the life of a character, using pictures at each time, and weaving the number into the story: for example, at 10:00 Mr Bean caught the Number 10 morning bus into town; at 14:00 he ate 14 beans on toast for his lunch; at 15:00 he had a cup of tea with 15 lumps of sugar in it … etc. The groups then shared their stories with the class. At the end of the lesson, they spontaneously applauded Sam and Ed for leading the lesson.

Q: What evidence of learning does this scenario suggest? What role would Ed and Sam's teacher have played in this learning? What role would peers have played?

Scenario 3a: Classroom displays

Class 5J has a total of 10 display boards (some double) around the classroom. These contain displays/information put up solely by the teacher or TA which consist of the following:

- Rewards points and names of 'monitors';
- Mounted samples of children's written work/pictures;
- Rules for English grammar;
- Rules for mathematical functions;
- Reminders for behaviour/conduct/rights and responsibilities;
- Number line and multiplication chart;
- Display relating to the class history topic created by teacher using some drawings by children and some commercially produced pictures and charts. A teaching assistant with an artistic flair has designed and cut out the display headings.

Q: What evidence of learning does this scenario suggest? What role would 5J's teacher have played in this learning? What role would peers have played?

Scenario 3b: Classroom displays

Class 5J has displays which are all designed and maintained by members of the class. The displays consist of the following:

- The class calendar for the year containing all birthdays, trips, events, holidays, etc. All around the calendar are photos of the pupils and teachers, with their families, pets, etc., which pupils have put up;

- Class notice board, with details of things to remember, lost and found, posters for class and school events, copies of recent newsletters;

- Class newspaper takes up four notice boards. This includes reports of sports and arts activities attended and participated in, recipes, stories, reviews of TV and music, articles on hobbies and local or national news items that have caught the interest of pupils;

- Two notice boards are 'work in progress' by a group of pupils who have been using Minecraft to explore Leonardo da Vinci designs and want to display some of their work for the class to see;

- One notice board has a display of food images and labels that a group of pupils is getting ready to use in a class session on healthy eating next week;

- On the class notice board there is a sheet of paper where individuals and groups (including teachers) can sign up for ideas for future displays. These ideas will be discussed and voted upon by the class in the weekly class meeting.

Q: What evidence of learning does this scenario suggest? What role would 5J's teacher have played in this learning? What role would peers have played?

Scenario 4a: Classroom environment

Mr F of Class 3F comes into school during the last week of the holiday to prepare his classroom for the new class. He lines all the display boards, puts names on all the trays and allocates each child a seat. He makes a library area next to the window and puts a jar of sharpened pencils and coloured crayons on each table. He wants everything to be really nice for the new class. When the new children arrive, they look for their names on trays and tables and put their belongings in trays and sit down to await their teacher's instructions.

Q: What evidence of learning does this scenario suggest? What role would Mr F have played in this learning? What role would peers have played?

Scenario 4b: Classroom environment

Mr F prepares his classroom for his new class. He puts all the books in boxes, puts the pencils (some need sharpening) scissors, rulers, etc. into boxes, and places all these on a table in the centre of the room. He stacks up all the chairs and tables. When the new children arrive, Mr F welcomes them and invites them to sit on the carpet with him (his chair is stacked with the others). He begins by saying that the first task they need to do is to find out about each other and then get their classroom sorted out together, and seeks ideas from pupils for how they might go about these tasks.

Q: What evidence of learning does this scenario suggest? What role would Mr F have played in this learning? What role would peers have played?

By writing these scenarios, a number of issues come up – one is the skills and organisation that would have to go into the transformation of classrooms into one of these; whether the learning is better in scenario b) than a); whether teachers believe that pupils would do a good enough job of teaching each other, and how much teacher input this would take. Unless the teacher has a belief in the importance of giving children responsibility and engaging them in this way, this would seem absurd. Maybe writing similar scenarios for parents might help:

Scenario 5a: Breakfast at Josh's house

Mum wakes Josh (9) up and tells him to get dressed – she has laid his clothes out for him and put the dirty ones he left on the floor in the laundry basket. He goes back to sleep so she goes up to wake him again and pours his coco pops out for him and makes his packed lunch. As he is eating breakfast she gets his swimming costume and towel into his PE bag and puts it by the door so he doesn't forget it.

Q: What evidence of learning does this scenario suggest? What role would Mum have played in this learning?

Scenario 5b: Breakfast at Josh's house

Josh (9) set his alarm early as he needs to get his stuff ready for swimming after school. He gets his stuff together in his PE bag and greets his Mum who is downstairs making coffee and they sit down together to eat breakfast. Over breakfast, Josh and Mum talk about what he might take for his packed lunch today and as she is clearing up the breakfast, Josh makes them both a packed lunch (they take it in turns to do this for each other).

Q: What evidence of learning does this scenario suggest? What role would Mum have played in this learning?

Now it's your turn. For your Scenario a, think back to a lesson you taught recently. Focus particularly on the decisions that you made on behalf of your pupils, and what preparation and follow-up you did for this lesson. Focus on decisions you made on behalf of the whole class, rather than about individuals, and also on the assumptions that you made about the pupils' skills, motivation and prior knowledge and experience.

Q: What evidence of learning does this scenario suggest? What role would you (and any other practitioners present) have played in this learning? What role would peers have played?

For your Scenario b, imagine what a future, more collaborative, version of this lesson might look like, using some of the characteristics of collaborative classrooms described in Chapter 7.

Be patient

Research shows that when a teacher begins to use CDM to engage pupils more actively in the classroom, improvements in their motivation may only start to show towards the end of that term, particularly for those pupils who were previously most demotivated. This seems to be because pupils who are unused to CDM need to experience several weeks of satisfying classroom experiences before they trust their teacher's new approach. They may doubt that their teacher is serious about letting them in on decision-making until they have had time to test their teacher out. On the other hand, if pupils perceive that they are just going to have the same experiences of teacher-control that turned them off learning in the past, they will switch off again very quickly. That is why it is important first of all to be sure that CDM is what you want to do in your school and classroom. Being open with pupils right from the start about what you are planning to do gives them time to get used to the idea, and means they will be more likely to trust that you really do mean to collaborate with them. Australian educator Garth Boomer called this 'coming clean'(Boomer, 1992).

Getting pupils on board

In a collaborative classroom the teacher's first job is to help the class to create an environment where everybody belongs and where it feels safe to ask questions, offer opinions and share ideas. This is true whether you are introducing CDM to pupils you already teach, or starting off with a new class. For teachers in secondary schools, with the pressures to cover a programme of study or exam syllabus, it can seem like a luxury to invest time in helping members of several classes to get to know each other and their teachers, and to develop a purposefully collaborative classroom culture. However, any time spent on this will pay back with dividends as pupils feel safe – more at ease with themselves and each other – releasing learning potential and creativity.

Some people say that once you've made up your mind to really involve pupils in decision-making that you need to be consistent and not just pick or choose to encourage participation in this subject and not for others. Don't let this put you off.

None of the three teachers who participated in my study (Rowe, 2018) was using CDM all of the time, which may be unsettling to those advocating a purist approach, but perhaps reassuring to those of you embarking on this as novices. It appeared from my study that pupils can be quite accepting of a mixed economy of collaborative and teacher-centric decision-making, but willingly rise to the occasion when asked to collaborate in decision-making. Once pupils feel safe to offer suggestions and to question established ways of doing things, teachers tell me that it is quite a relief not to always be the person to decide what to keep and what to change.

Teachers have introduced CDM into their classrooms in different ways. The three teachers who participated in my research followed highly personalised paths to classroom participation, reflecting their own circumstances, needs and interests.

Carl set out to develop a classroom where children would learn how to make decisions as a community by stepping back and encouraging the class to sort things out for themselves. But first, he paid attention to developing a classroom culture where pupils felt free to say anything in class without fear of getting it wrong or appearing foolish.

Michael also set out to build a classroom culture where children felt safe and had a great deal of fun in lessons, but his natural approach was to teach pupils the necessary skills before he let go of the reins. Unlike Carl, the vision he had of his ideal classroom did not initially include pupils making decisions as a class, nor having a hand in designing the curriculum. These things were happening from time to time, but not as part of a plan to empower pupils. Michael's motivation for CDM came from his wish to be open and honest with his pupils about the decisions that he was making on their behalf. He also held a strong belief that decisions should be made by those most affected by them.

My third participant, Philip, had great rapport with his class and said that he had always found it very easy to hold conversations with them and talk about their mutual interests. However, it was through being sent on training as a teacher–facilitator for a philosophy-based whole class intervention that he became aware of his pupils' potential for sophisticated thinking and decision-making. The generalisation of the in-depth class conversations and debates evolved as Philip stood back more and more and handed decision-making power to his pupils.

Some teachers find that 'coming clean' with your class right from the start is important – letting them know that you're going to involve them in decision-making, and why, and what this might look like (Shor, 1996). Others prefer to test the waters with some 'light touch' low-risk activities. So, alongside building the culture, doing some CDM with pupils and then reflecting on it may be the easiest way to start: how did they feel about it? What do they like about making decisions together? Why did it work? What other things could we decide together?

You might want to look at the classroom stories in this book and see if there are any approaches you could adapt for yourself. Alternatively, you may want to copy some stories from this book to discuss with your class, and together agree how you might start to use CDM in your own lessons. Pupils really seem to like it when their teachers give the message, 'We're all in this together.' However, there can be some suspicion, reluctance or even outright resistance to CDM from some pupils, usually in schools with a highly competitive or authoritarian culture, which is why good preparation at both the personal and institutional level is really important.

Any move in the direction of increasing collaboration with pupils, however small, is positive. Don't be in too much of a hurry to move on, before reflecting on the experience with pupils, analysing together what difference the new collaboration made, and discussing ways to sustain and improve on classroom practice. For example, if you have involved pupils in deciding how to celebrate the end of term, reflect with them how this was done, what difference it made to be involved, how it felt to have a say and what they have learnt about themselves and others as a result. This 'communal metacognition' around participation is an invaluable opportunity for pupils' cognitive, emotional and social development and time spent on this kind of discussion will greatly strengthen learning and cohesion in the class.

For example, a class who have collaborated with their teacher on planning an assembly may decide they would like to have more of a say about the school trip; pupils who have had input on redesigning spelling tests may want to change the way times tables are learnt and assessed.

Consider moving collaboration further up the decision-making hierarchy, so that pupils gradually become more involved in decisions around policy. If you have already successfully involved pupils in deciding how the teacher can reduce the noise in a classroom, then you may wish to involve pupils in deciding how they themselves can monitor and have some control over classroom noise levels.

The challenges pupils present

The *fear* of personal criticism from pupils, expressed by teachers who have not used CDM themselves, does not appear to materialise in practice. Perhaps the teachers who choose CDM have already decided not to take criticism personally or, through showing trust in pupils, this trust has been reciprocated. What does emerge from teachers' stories is that there may always be pupils who either hold back from participation or actively resist it. White and Gunstone quote Baird and Mitchell's (1986) description of the occasion where two pupils came to their science teacher to express dismay at his invitation to participate in decision-making:

> 'We see what all this is about now,' one said. 'You are trying to get us to think and learn for ourselves.' 'Yes, yes,' replied the teacher, heartened by this long-delayed breakthrough, 'that's it exactly.' 'Well,' said the student, 'We don't want to do that.'
>
> (White & Gunstone, 1989)

One Languages teacher using CDM reasoned that pupils may sometimes see tasks that are 'unfamiliar' as 'harder', and so prefer to revert to the passive roles they are more used to, or even try to get the teacher to revert to a more authoritarian role (Moreno-Lopez, 2005). When teachers start to use CDM, they perceive that pupils can be confused as to who is responsible for certain things and may even blame the teacher's change of role if they forget to do things, such as hand in their home work (Moreno-Lopez, 2005).

Teachers have found their own ways of transitioning from a more authoritarian into a more collaborative role: by changing the nature of classroom talk from day one of a new course of study, discussing the syllabus and how the course might be assessed (Shor, 1996); by having one task or issue each lesson where new forms of collaboration are explicitly encouraged (Mazur, 1997); or by discussing openly with pupils the dilemma the teacher has with moving from one role to another (Hannam, 2020). Teacher Ira Shor described the need to carry out a 'transition' phase for pupils not ready to take on this new pedagogy of CDM. It has also been suggested that teachers may need to identify pupils who continue to need a higher level of teacher support and reassurance in a democratic classrooms than their peers (Rogers, 1983).

Teachers in Dr Eve Mayes' study of schools in Melbourne, Australia, were disappointed to find that the rate of progress of pupil voice in their schools was slower than they had expected (Mayes, Finneran, & Black, 2018). They put this down not to pupils' lack of skill, but that pupils and teachers needed to trust each other more. Pupils themselves had an insight into why some of their peers held back, saying that some pupils need much more persistent encouragement from the teacher to join in, and some might just be daydreaming. Pupils felt strongly that pupils who misbehaved really needed to be listened to if they were to change their ways.

So, we need to be ready to respond when pupils fail to take up the opportunities to give their views or collaborate in decision-making. Their reluctance or resistance can be understood if we consider that it's possible that pupils:

- Have weak perception of their own power to make changes and influence decisions;
- Are not yet confident that the adults will respect and act on their views, to take them as seriously as other adults;

- Don't yet believe that their voice will make a difference;
- Are not sure what is expected of them; they are so used to doing what the teacher tells them to do;
- Are uncertain about how what they say will be received or treated. For example, how confidential their comments are;
- Lack confidence in articulating their views and wants;
- Don't believe that fellow pupils will take CDM seriously;
- Have little or no experience of CDM at home or in previous classes;
- Perceive themselves to have lower status than others (especially true of children from economically deprived homes) (The Sutton Trust, 2019); or
- Worry about offending their teachers.

Solutions suggested by Eve's team of researchers and teachers in their study included:

- Use older pupils to facilitate discussions and decision-making in the classrooms of younger pupils;
- Train teachers in how to bring less confident pupils into discussions;
- Start with small groups;
- Ensure that the pupils who are most in need of having a voice a chance to speak up (including those whose conduct is troublesome or have poor attendance) – or else they will most likely go on misbehaving and missing school;
- Discuss the importance of feedback and have joint training for teachers and pupils on giving and receiving feedback;
- Talk about why feedback is important and practice different ways of giving and receiving feedback.

Parents

Teachers sometimes ask me how they might describe CDM to parents who might find this whole idea confusing or even preposterous! Hopefully, if this is a whole school approach, then proactive steps will have been taken to communicate the school culture to parents, explaining what the school's values are and how these will look like in practice. I like the whole idea of asking the pupils' advice about how to communicate CDM to their parents – they know their own parents better than you do, and know what will or will not appeal to them. All three participants in my research got highly positive feedback from parents, especially from those whose children had previously felt disengaged or unsuccessful, but who were now investing much more of themselves in class and the school community. Although each of these teachers told me that they did worry that if parents had a child in one class using CDM another in a class with no CDM they might find this confusing, none of the teachers had actually experienced this. Once again, if a collaborative ethos is embraced by the whole school, this problem will not arise.

In my experience, some of the best examples of existing CDM are between parents and teachers. I've seen successful negotiations on how homework will be given and completed; ways of addressing problematic attendance; and many other examples of great collaboration between teachers and parents to resolve issues of friendship and academic issues. When pupils are involved in these discussions and decision-making, the outcomes are almost invariably even better.

Lone teachers

Teachers I have come across who use CDM in their teaching, usually with the full support of their head teachers, have all been working in schools where they were the only teacher teaching in this way. This can leave teachers open to conflict with colleagues and little hope that their investment with the class will be followed up or built upon in the next class, along with other aspects of the school culture which made it challenging to work in this way.

I mentioned earlier that reports from my research participants, and from other teachers who have used CDM in conventional schools, suggest that the biggest problems they face are not from the children but from colleagues and from aspects of the school culture that do not support, or may even discourage, collaboration. Whilst all three of my participants had head teachers who were highly supportive of their use of CDM, they found that this encouragement was not backed up by a collaborative school ethos. This meant that not only were colleagues sometimes fearful or suspicious of these teachers' CDM, but that there was nobody they could go to when they needed guidance on what to do when things were not going well. They also identified the lack of teacher voice in their schools, which maybe contributed to their colleagues' lack of motivation for collaboration with pupils.

Maths teacher Susan Hyde, whose story you will have read in Chapter 6, found that colleagues' responses to her collaborative teaching were highly varied. Whilst some were interested and fully supportive, others were highly critical of the raised noise levels caused by class discussions and the lack of uniformity in what pupils were doing. Whilst these criticisms could have been stressful, Hyde also saw them as the opportunity to practice articulating a theory and objectives for her practice, which she considered no bad thing (Hyde, 1992).

As well as criticisms from colleagues who do not understand, or who disagree with the reasoning behind giving pupils a say in classroom decisions, other more subtle influences can be at work on non-authoritarian teachers. Newly qualified teachers for the most part feel they are successful when they feel they 'fit in' with their colleagues. As it is still quite rare to find teachers sharing decision-making with their pupils on a regular basis, any newcomer who does so will soon notice the discrepancy between what they and their colleagues are doing, and feel a pressure to conform to established school practices, that do not align with their own values. A good example of this is the school behaviour policy. Across the age range, pupils experience systems of 'behaviour management' where every teacher is required to

> 'The sense of isolation for many teachers who embody non-mainstream sentiments can be quite taxing.'
> Landon Beyer, Director of Teacher Education, decrying the lack of support for innovative teaching.'
> (Beyer, 1996)

make value judgements about the behaviour of individuals or groups of pupils and mete out punishments and rewards accordingly. Teachers who feel uncomfortable with adopting such whole-school practices often feel under great pressure to go along with the practices, or at least give the impression to colleagues that they are doing so, to avoid ridicule or rejection. I read about one teacher who felt that there was a very strong message in her school culture: 'conform, perform, and be uniform' (Beyer, 1996).

Building bridges

Anyone wanting to make changes in an educational system, and in schools in particular, has to be aware of the many entrenched authoritarian cultural aspects that underpin many established school and classroom practices. Boomer makes the point that this makes it almost impossible for a single teacher to make much difference to the underlying authoritarianism in a school – it needs to be a whole-school venture!

However, if you find yourself on your own, search out colleagues within your school and in other schools with whom you can collaborate, sharing and reflecting on each other's experiences of CDM. If you are to model collaboration to your pupils, you need to expand your own personal experiences of CDM. Build bridges with other colleagues by showing an interest in *them*. If you spend time finding out about what your colleagues are doing and why, without criticising or talking about your own practice, you are laying the foundations for a good relationship that will eventually lead to their being more accepting of, and even interested in, your approaches. The same is true for your relationships with colleagues as with pupils: you are most influential when you *listen*, not when you *speak* (Glasser, 1988).

To summarise, lone teachers need to first build relationships and bridges with colleagues, then be bold and different and 'rock the boat' with your CDM, encouraging your colleagues and school leaders to do the same.

I hope that after reading this chapter, you feel positive and confident you can try CDM. Be prepared for some initial puzzlement from children and parents. Be patient; pupils' acceptance of, and active participation in collaboration may only really show itself by the end of term. Keep going back to the pupils to talk things through – don't feel you have to resort to the old habits, even though others might counsel against further collaboration. Keep a CDM journal – or even better, get pupils to write it! Share your own joys and worries with each other – otherwise you are removing the collaborative nature of the enterprise.

References

Beyer, L. E.. (Ed.) (1996). *Creating democratic classrooms: the struggle to integrate theory and practice.* New York: Teachers College Press.

Boomer, G. (1992). *Negotiating the curriculum: Educating for the 21st century* (pp. 4–14). London and New York: Routledge.

Cook-Sather, A. (2007). What would happen if we treated students as those with opinions tha tmatter? The benefits to principals and teachers of supporting youth engagement in school. *NASSP Bulletin, 91*(4), 343–362. Retrieved from https://doi.org/10.1177/0192636507309872.

Davies, L., Williams, C., Yamashita, H., & Man-hing, K. (2005). *Inspiring schools – impact and outcomes: Taking up the challenge of pupil participation.* London: Carnegie Young People Initiative & Esmée Fairbairn Foundation.

Fielding, M. (2010). Whole school meetings and the development of radical democratic community. *Studies in Philosophy and Education.* Retrieved from DOI: https://doi.org/10.1007/s11217-010-9208-5

Flutter, J., & Rudduck, J. (2004). *Consulting pupils: What's in it for schools?* London: Routledge Falmer.

Glasser, W. (1988). *Choice theory in the classroom* (revised). New York: Harper.

Glasser, W. (2000). School violence from the perspective of William Glasser. *Professional School Counseling, 4*(2), 77–80.

Hannam, D. (2020). *Another Way is Possible - Becoming a Democratic Teacher in a State School.* ebook: Smashwords.

Hyde, S. (1992). Sharing power in the classroom. In G. Boomer, C. Onore, N. Lester, & J. Cook. (Eds.), *Negotiating the curriculum: Educating for the 21st century* (pp. 67–77)). Abingdon, UK: Routledge Falmer.

Mayes, E., Finneran, R., & Black, R. (2018). Victorian student representative council (VicSRC) primary school engagement (PSE) evaluation final evaluation report PSE. Melbourne: Victorian Student Representative Council (VicSRC) Retrieved from https://www.academia.edu/41223522/Victorian_Student_Representative_Council_VicSRC_Primary_School_Engagement_PSE_Evaluation_Final_Evaluation_report_PSE_-December_2018

Mazur, E. (1997). Peer Instruction: A User's Manual. Upper Saddle River, NJ: Prentice Hall.

Mills, C. W. (1959). *The sociological imagination.* New York: Oxford University Press.

Moreno, L. I. (2005). Sharing Power with Students: The critical language classroom. *Radical Pedagogy, 7*(2). Retrieved from http://radicalpedagogy.icaap.org/content/issue7_2/moreno.html

Rowe, G. (2018) Democracy in the primary classroom. Unpublished thesis. UCL Institute of Education. Retrieved from: www.pupilparticipation.co.uk/resources

Ryan, R. M., & Deci, E. L. (2000). Self-determination theory and the facilitation of intrinsic motivation, social development, and well-being. *American Psychologist, 55*(1), 68–78.

Shier, H. (2006). Pathways to participation revisited. *Dialogue and Debate,* (2), 14–19. Retrieved from http://www.harryshier.net/docs/Shier-Pathways_to_Participation_Revisited_NZ2006.pdf

Shor, I. (1996). *When students have power.* Chicago, IL: TheUniversity of Chicago Press. Retrieved from https://books.google.co.uk/books?id=L4_eBQAAQBAJ&pg=PA30&lpg=PA30&dq=inaugurate+a+new+speech+community&source=bl&ots=DIcuI8Et9m&sig=sYFB4WV7fNpc0aWINEitZjE6Yjo&hl=en&sa=X&ved=0ahUKEwiaupG6wYHKAhWB0RoKHTIsBmsQ6AEIHzAA#v=onepage&q&f=false

The Sutton Trust (2019). *Elitist Britain.* London: The Sutton Trust with The Social Mobility Commission.

White, R. T., & Gunstone, R. F. (1989). Metalearning and Conceptual Change. *International Journal of Science Education, 11*(5), 577–586.

Wilson, S. (2002). Student participation and school culture: A secondary school case study. *Australian Journal of Education, 46*(1), 79–102. Retrieved from https://doi.org/10.1177/000494410204600107.

Conclusion

To close this book, I want to make some points about initial teacher education and educational policy, well aware that I have limited personal experience in these areas. However, I have worked alongside teachers and head teachers for over 30 years and observed the changes in teacher education over that time. As an Educational Psychologist, I have experienced the impact of the education policies of six governments, and closely observed the effect these policies have had on school leaders, teachers and pupils.

Implications for policymakers

As I write this concluding chapter, schools all around the world have shut their doors, and in the UK alone, in this second week of self-isolation, millions of parents are struggling to educate their children at home. We do not know how long the coronavirus measures will go on for. What we do know is that when schools reopen things will be different. Parents are getting a taste of the challenge of teaching their own children. Some are enjoying it, some are going mad trying and others have abandoned any attempts to even keep their offspring at home.

The reopening of our schools offers a great opportunity for change. When pupils return they will have had months out of the classroom. School leaders have options. Either they can make plans to return to the previous culture, which may involve re-institutionalising children into compliance and acceptance of the 'pre-corona' values, or they can look at the amazing collaboration that is proving so vital to the community during these difficult times, and plan to make that sense of collaboration and community a real feature of the school.

If you decide the latter, as I hope you will, then there need to be changes in the whole system to support schools to do this. Whether you are reading this book following the coronavirus crisis, or many years later, your decision to become a more collaborative school will need support from the wider education system. For schools to develop a collaborative culture, governments need to look at their educational policies and examine whether they promote competition or collaboration between and within schools.

In the introduction, I proposed that CDM be expected, respected, inspected and invested in. The right kinds of inspection, training and resources need to be in place to support schools to be more collaborative, both within their own establishments, as described in this book, and also between schools, and between schools and government education departments.

In the UK, a recently updated framework for the inspection of schools places a priority on manageable workload and greater freedom for teachers to design and deliver a curriculum which allows pupils to explore their own talents and make the most of their interests and ambitions. This gives school staff an opportunity to involve pupils more fully in the design of their own schools and classrooms. This updated approach has the potential to encourage school leaders to have an ambitious and inclusive vision. The examples and suggestions in this book offer practical and realistic ways of meeting such an ambitious vision. I am concerned that not all school inspectors will recognise collaboration when they see it, and may even inadvertently discourage school leaders from taking steps towards greater CDM if schools get judged harshly by inspectors who do not understand the demands and rewards of a collaborative school ethos.

If schools are to enable teachers and pupils to negotiate the curriculum, then school leaders also need the space for this – something that can only happen if school staff have the freedom and skills to develop their own curriculum. Once again, this will only come about if policymakers themselves understand and value CDM as an educational philosophy.

Teacher education and professional development

Initial teacher education and preparation is increasingly based in schools and therefore relies on existing teachers acting as mentors to teacher trainees. Newly qualified teachers tell me that they are facing strong pressure to 'fit in' with existing practice. In order to be seen as succeeding, pupil teachers may feel the need to comply with some less-than-collaborative practices of their host schools as a survival strategy. New teachers will need preparation and support to challenge the status quo in schools where they are learning, if teachers of the future are to be champion collaboration.

Now is the time for the kind of professional development opportunities for teachers and school leaders that enable them to come together to devise new, collaborative approaches, and to support and learn from each other as they move into a new, more collaborative, era of schooling.

Index

*Note: Page numbers in **boldface** type indicate headings.*